ENDORSEMENTS

If you want your life radically transformed, then read *TAP* cover to cover. Get ready to see supernatural miracles manifested, to hear God's voice more clearly, and to change the atmosphere wherever you go! Shawn shares deep revelation and principles that will radically change your life and those around you.

After reading this book, I know my life will never be the same!

JANIE DUVALL
Speaker/music composer/TV producer
Former producer of Sid Roth's *It's Supernatural!*

TAP is an interesting and thought-provoking book. It will challenge your walk with God, open your eyes to the supernatural, and draw you to the Holy One. It contains Shawn Morris' journey into the supernatural, as well as principles that can change your life. Read it now, and start *TAPping* into the power of God for your life.

JOAN HUNTER
Author/evangelist
President, Joan Hunter Ministries

Shawn Morris' new book *TAP* is an inspirational testimonial. *TAP* will help the reader to *tap* into the Kingdom.

KEVIN BASCONI
Author
President, King of Glory International Ministries

If you are serious about the prophetic realm and want to understand how to live and operate in your prophetic gifting, then this is the book you need.

KATHIE WALTERS
Good News Ministries

This is a great book on the anointing of God and how it operates. I highly recommend this written work of Prophet Shawn Morris, led of and totally anointed by the Holy Spirit. I totally endorse this book written by a mighty, true prophet of God. It has truly inspired my life. This book is a must for this generation, and I would fully recommend it to all ministers of the Gospel. All churches should use this mighty book as a teaching aid for their classes. Prophet Shawn is a mighty man of prayer and moves in the anointing of the Holy Spirit; he is related to William J. Seymour of the Azusa Street Revival. He is truly of a godly heritage. The power of God rules his life.

GLENDA JACKSON

If you really want to know someone, travel with them, especially in Israel. As I spent time with Prophet Shawn Morris on such a tour and in later meetings, I quickly saw he is the real deal. He walks what he talks and he talks what he walks. That's true integrity. In the book *TAP*, you meet the man who teaches with both his words and his actions. In this highly confessional work, you will see how each principle has been worked out in his life and his ministry. This book is a treasure trove of tried and true principles for walking and working in the glory of God. I know these principles will enrich your walk as you apply them in your spirit, soul, and body.

JAMES DURHAM
Author/pastor
President, Higher Calling Ministries

TAP is a book that will help readers learn in further depth their identities in Christ and how to operate fully in the supernatural realm to advance the Kingdom of God on earth. I believe you will be richly blessed by the history and insight in this book.

Munday Martin
Contagious Love International Ministries

How to TAP *into the*

GLORY
of GOD

How to TAP into the
GLORY of GOD

Anointed Principles that Unlock
GOD'S POWER IN YOUR LIFE

SHAWN MORRIS

DESTINY IMAGE® PUBLISHERS, INC.
P.O. Box 310, Shippensburg, PA 17257-0310
"Promoting Inspired Lives."

Previously published as *TAP: The Anointed Principles*
Previous ISBN: 978-0615895062

This book and all other Destiny Image and Destiny Image Fiction books are available at Christian bookstores and distributors worldwide.

Cover design by Eileen Rockwell
Interior design by Terry Clifton

For more information on foreign distributors, call 717-532-3040.
Reach us on the Internet: www.destinyimage.com.

ISBN 13 TP: 978-0-7684-1195-9
ISBN 13 eBook: 978-0-7684-1196-6
ISBN 13 LP: 978-0-7684-1540-7
ISBN 13 HC: 978-0-7684-1541-4

For Worldwide Distribution, Printed in the U.S.A.
1 2 3 4 5 6 7 8 / 21 20 19 18 17

DEDICATION

This

book

is

dedicated

to

"The Lost and the Suffering Body of Christ."

TAP!

ACKNOWLEDGMENTS

First, I would love to acknowledge my God for ruling and reigning over my life. Second, I would love to honor and acknowledge Jesus Christ—my Lord, my Savior, my King, my Big Brother, my Friend, and my God. Without you, I never would have made it. Thank you once again for saving my soul. Third, I would love to honor one of the most important people in my life, one whom very few acknowledge. Yes, you Holy Spirit. You're my Teacher, my Comforter, my Advisor, and my tour Guide through life. Without you, I would be lost in this fallen world. Thank you for being the voice of reason in a realm of uncertainty.

To my wife, Tora, you are the most beautiful and anointed woman I have ever met. I thank God daily for bringing you into my life and into this ministry. When I found you, I knew I was a blessed man. Thank you for being my partner, my intercessor, my watchman, my soul mate, and my best friend. Thanks for motivating me and believing in me even when I didn't believe in myself. We are Bonnie and Clyde in the spirit realm. Love you always. Remember, we cannot lose.

I would like to give honor to those who mentored me along my journey: Pastor Benny Hinn, Tony Kemp, Bishop Lester Love, James Durham, Pastor Manuel Mukes, Dr. E. Woodie Mathis, David Herzog, and Sid Roth, from whom I learned a lot about the supernatural by being a faithful archive watcher of his television broadcast. These people were the instruments God used for my progress in the spiritual realm. I'm ever so grateful for you all.

A final acknowledgment goes out to my SMI family. I want to thank Evangelist J.J. Simmons for leading me to the Lord and for pushing me to write this book. Thanks for being a lifetime friend and brother. See you at the top. To Justin and Rachael Eldred of AHOP Ministries for supporting this project—you are the best protégés any mentor could have. And last but not least, I would like to acknowledge Angela Trippi for being a huge part of this ministry's success. Thanks for helping me type up and preedit the book. I thank God for sending me such a humble servant of Christ. Keep up the good work. This is just the beginning. We cannot lose!

PROPHET SHAWN MORRIS

CONTENTS

FOREWORD

Shawn is one of those unusual persons who experiences supernatural occurrences and manifestations of grace in their lives and ministries because of the goodness of God and the presence of the Lord Jesus Christ. Through his desire to know the person of God the Father, he has been given the ability to receive divine revelations that bring about visible manifestations of the presence of Jesus in the present. As you read the pages of this book, your hunger for the Lord Jesus will be increased. Your thirst for the Spirit and the anointing of God will be deepened, and your understanding of how to TAP into the anointing of God will be sharpened. You will be able to experience Jesus in ways you have never had before.

The revelation of the word that Shawn shares will enable you to see, hear, and know Jesus at the level where you can release the anointing and the power of God. As the light of God shines upon your spirit and soul, you will learn how to make Jesus known to others and bring heaven to earth so others can experience both the love and the life of the living God. Jesus said, "*Unless you see signs and wonders, you will not believe.*" This "*show me generation*" must see signs, wonders, and miracles that are so profound in the natural that they will be led to genuine repentance, sincere faith, and deep intimacy with the Lord Jesus. Through *How to TAP into the Glory of God*, you will find information, inspiration, revelation, manifestation, and ultimate glorification of the Lord Jesus.

Dear follower of God, it is time for you to arise and shine for your light has come, and the glory of the Lord has risen upon you. Be prepared to enter into His light and His glory. As you read the pages of this book, may you know Jesus more intimately and manifest Him more evidently in your life and ministry. To God be the glory!

PASTOR TONY KEMP
President of Tony Kemp Ministries and Embassy Christian Center
Hannibal, Missouri

THE AVONSHIRE REVIVAL

The following historical event took place at a house church on the southwest side of Houston, Texas. The event received no public attention, but it should have been written down in the history books as one of the greatest house revivals of modern times.

These true events took place in 2010 in my living room at 13319 Avonshire Street. I had a burning desire for a revival to come to my city. I had no experience or education on the subject, so I started a journey to study and discover the recipe for a great awakening. My wife and I wanted more than just a Sunday routine week after week. We wanted God!

I started a Bible study in my house that gradually grew into a small house church. In the early days of the church meetings, all I would preach was repentance. The Lord used me often to prophesy over the people, and they would tell their friends to "Come and see this pastor who has told me about my whole life." The church grew to a good solid twenty members. As long as I was prophesying, the people stayed.

However, when the Lord started telling me to preach on sin issues, church membership dwindled. On one Sunday in particular, no one showed up. It was just my wife, our children, and I in attendance. I was discouraged and devastated. I felt like I had let God and my family down. However, my wife urged me to preach to her and the kids like they were the crowd. Even though it was encouraging what my wife said, I needed new direction and I needed it fast.

THE NEXT MOVE

The church was dismantled, but I had to pull myself together. I made up in my mind that God had promised me revival, so I wasn't going to stop seeking Him until I received it. I was like Jacob wrestling with the angel for the blessing. So, I went on Sid Roth's *It's Supernatural!* website, and I found a show in his archives about the Azusa Street Revival. The author of the book was Tommy Welchel, and the name of the book was *They Told Me Their Stories*. It was about the youth who had been used by God at the great Azusa Street Revival. I went to purchase the book online from Sid Roth's website, but there were no more in stock.

I went to Tommy Welchel's website, and it directed me to buy the book from the printer. The name of the man who printed the book was Dr. J. Edward Morris. I found it ironic that we both shared the same last name. To top it off, he lived in Houston as well. I told the Lord, "You must be doing something here." Dr. Morris and I quickly became good friends. We went out to lunch, and he took my wife and me to his house. He gave us two copies of the book. He kept insisting that I needed to write a book. However, I just wanted to read about how these anointed people had ushered in a revival.

As I read the book, my faith skyrocketed to another level. I longed to see those kinds of miracles in my own life. I had the anointing at the time to a certain degree, but it wasn't on the scale that this book was referring to. I knew I need to see more of what the Lord had to offer. I wasn't satisfied with a small portion of His presence and power. I wanted the fullness of His Spirit or nothing at all.

ANSWERED PRAYERS

Several weeks passed, and I read the book over and over again. I would cry out at the altar in our living room for the Spirit to move like He did at Azusa Street. I told the Lord I didn't want the burden of revival if it wasn't like Azusa or better. I didn't even want to do the work of the ministry anymore if His presence didn't manifest. It became a relentless desperation to see revival. I was no longer a pastor at that point; I had conformed into a fire-filled revivalist.

We began to invite people out for our monthly revival meetings at the house. Many came because they didn't feel obligated to join our house church. In Houston, if you didn't have a building then you weren't a church. One day, I was led to do a three-day dry fast, which included no water and no food; we called it the "Esther fast." My wife was running last-minute errands before the meeting, and she left me alone in the house so I could seek the Lord.

I lay prostrate on the floor and tried to enter into the Holy of Holies. I started to fall asleep, and I heard a voice say, "Tonight revival is coming." I remained on the floor and saw visions of clouds. My eyes were closed, and my body went numb as I saw a bright light. All of a sudden, my wife walked in the door and said, "What have you done?"

I opened my eyes and responded, "What did I do?" The house was full of a thick mist that covered the entire floor. We thought someone left something on the stove burning because the entire house was foggy. I got up to see it clearly, and as soon as I raised my hand, my wife flew across the room. She fell every time I went near her. This is something we never experienced before. I knew in my spirit something had been released to us, but *what* was the big question. That night, I was waiting to see what would happen. I knew my wife had felt the power of God, but what about the people's reactions? I didn't know how long the fog would remain. I was thinking maybe it's just my wife who's being affected by it. I did feel very sensitive to the spirit as I have in the past. However, this time my eyes and ears were clearer than usual and the visual manifestation of the fog in my house totally blew my mind. At that moment, I had no idea what was taking place and the fear of the fog lifting had me nervous that whole day.

It was 7:00 on a Friday night; people began to arrive at our home. Some could barely see because of the cloud; the mist was still in our midst. People were slain in the Spirit as they walked through the front door. They were not even hurt as they fell forward to the marble floor on their faces. I had seen people fall backward before, but never forward. It was all new to me. Many would fall from their chairs as I preached messages of repentance. Some couldn't get off the floor because their legs where weighed down by the Shekinah glory that filled the house. That night I knew we had called down revival and my prayers were finally answered. The first few days into the revival, no one could come close to me because I had extreme heat and glory that pulsated from my body. My wife made me sleep on the couch just so she could rest. I stayed up for three days and three nights straight with no sleep. I asked the Lord could He please let it lift off of me or else I was going to die. The glory was so strong that I had electrical waves racing through my body every thirty minutes. My eyes were so dilated they thought I might have to be admitted into a hospital. However, on the fourth day of the revival the Lord lifted the anointing off of me so I could function normally again.

For months, oil from heaven dripped from our ceiling in all our rooms. People wouldn't leave the meetings until four or five in the morning. Gold dust appeared inside and outside of the cars that lined up on our street. It would cover the faces of the people, especially the children. People were getting healed of all kinds of incurable diseases. Many would levitate off the ground during deliverance services. Cancerous tumors would fall from people's bodies unto the floor. Those in wheelchairs would get up with no hesitation. Every healing and miracle came with ease. Many healings took place without us even laying on a finger. The atmosphere was so anointed that as soon as you walked through the door, whatever you needed would manifest instantly. Angel feathers would fall from midair during our children's meetings in the morning. I believe the Lord gave them that manifestation because they were so innocent. Neighbors reported seeing a cloudy mist around our house at all times during the day. At some of the meetings, people said they saw rainbows and flashes of light by our pulpit. Many reported that they saw fire come out my mouth when I preached. I never saw it myself, but others did. It would actually rain inside the house when we worshiped God. Many people went into trances and had heavenly visitations. It was like heaven invaded our home.

People came from other cities to see the manifestation and movement of God at our little house church. What made it interesting was the fact that we had no promotional team, no flyers to advertise—we were not even on social media at that time. Everything was done by word of mouth. Conviction was so heavy that homosexual men and women would get converted instantly and start speaking in tongues. Cross-dressers would come back the next day dressed up in the clothing of their gender. Men would dress like men and women would dress like women. There would never be a dry eye at alter call; even during my message people would break out into a travail and I couldn't finish the sermon. A heavy sense of conviction and longing for God was in that place.

The Lord also used the youth to prophesy. My eleven-year-old daughter Ida would stand in front of people and call out accurate words of knowledge. Grown men and women would fall down and burst into tears because of the accuracy of the prophetic word. There were miracles of instant weight loss; money appeared in bank accounts, purses, and wallets; and many miraculous healings and heavenly visitations took place. God visited us in powerful ways. My prayers had been answered. Revival had arrived, but how long would it stay? That was the question that haunted me the whole duration of the revival. As much faith I had during the revival to operate in miracles, the thought of it lifting was my biggest fear.

THE FIRE FADES

The revival on Avonshire Street lasted about eight to nine months. Myself and my wife being young in the faith, we allowed a few so-called seasoned pastors to come in and help us with the revival. We were looking for spiritual mentors who could help us understand what we had TAPped into. So, they came in and tried to bring order and structure to the meetings. They would pressure us about getting a building. They wanted us to become more organized. So, I began to try to get more structured and organized like

I was told by theses wise elders in the faith. Once this took place, the fog begin to diminish, the healings slowed down, the attendance dwindled, and even prophecy began to fade. No one understood how it came or how it went. However, my wife and I knew. The media never got involved or covered the story. However, those who were touched by it will never forget its impact. The landlord and the neighborhood association banned us from having meetings in the house. They said we were operating a commercial business in a residential area, so they shut us down. The truth of the matter was, the neighbors got upset with us because people were parking in their parking spaces during the revival. The AC unit and many other household appliances started to break down, and the oil that dripped from the ceiling dried up. It was over; the fire had faded, and any hope of it spreading worldwide proved to be a pipe dream. During the revival, many prophets came and prophesied that we were carriers of revival. One prophet said I had the mantle of William J. Seymour, not knowing that I had been studying about him prior to the Avonshire revival.

Prophetess Glenda Jackson, who is the niece of Maria Woodworth-Etter, told me that one day she was reading my book and God told her Prophet Shawn was the descendant of William J. Seymour of the Azusa Street Revival. She said the Lord told her that I carried the one-hundred-year prophesy that was spoken by Seymour around 1910. She said revival would come out through my ministry to fulfill the prophecy of my ancestors. When Prophetess Glenda shared this with me, the Holy Spirit hit me like a lightning bolt. I was struck by the power of God, and waves of glory went through my body. Other prophets had said that to me before, but when this woman of God said it the Lord confirmed the word with signs following. I saw why the Lord gave us such grace. I was a part of the revival bloodline of God's generals, just like Glenda. Even though the Avonshire revival wasn't on the level of Azusa Street, the Holy Spirit graced us with a taste of what was to come. If the Lord had allowed me to experience that measure of His Spirit at Avonshire when I was spiritually immature, imagine what would happen in the days to come as we began to TAP into the wells of revival.

Lord, I pray that you pour out your Spirit in great measure. Open up the closed wells of the revival of our ancestors and send water to a dry and thirsty land. Send conviction to the lost sheep, and help us turn from our wicked ways. Allow the prophecies of God's generals, like William J. Seymour and others, to come to pass now! We receive revival, renewal, restructure, restoration, and awakening in Jesus' name.

WHAT IS TAP?

Let's break down the meaning of TAP.

TAP stands for *The Anointed Principles* of God. These anointed principles are a gift of God's glory or unction to move in His glory. The word *gift* is translated from the Greek word *charisma*, which means "grace endowment" or "undeserved favor" or "spiritual gift."[1]

We may be wondering, just what is an endowment? Well, to endow is to supply with a permanent income or income-producing property.[2] A gift is an investment or endowment from the Lord that constantly produces income. As we work with the Lord, we will see a resulting increase. We work *for* the Lord and *with* the Lord to produce fruit in the earthly realm.

In Matthew 25:14-15, we see the following Scripture:

> *For the kingdom of heaven is as a man traveling into a far country, who called his own servants, and delivered unto them his goods. And unto one he gave **five** talents, to another **two**, and to another **one**; to every man according to his several ability; and straightway took his journey.*

In this parable, Jesus explains how different people receive different measures or amounts of the anointing. Many people think we all have the same level of anointing, gifts, or talents. For example, in Ephesians 4:8, the Scripture says, *"Wherefore he saith. When he ascended up on high, he led the captivity captive, and gave gifts unto men."* Verse 11 of the same passage lists the gifts He gave: *"And he gave some, apostles; and some, prophets; and some, evangelists and some, pastors and teachers"* (Eph. 4:11). Notice that the writer used the word *some*, not *all*. Also notice he named five gifts, just like the five talents Jesus mentioned in Matthew 25:15: *"And unto one he gave five talents, to another two, and to another one; to every man according to his several ability."* The biblical meaning of the number five is grace, which is the enabling power of God.[3] I believe the five talents in this parable represent the five-fold ministry of Jesus that Paul wrote about in Ephesians 4:8-11.

It says in Matthew 25:15, it was *"according to his several ability."* *Ability* is defined as possessing the necessary qualities to carry out an action. It can also mean "competence, skill, or a particular talent." Wow! So this coincides with the parable of the talents. Everyone doesn't have the same talent or gift. However, some can move in all five, some in two, and some in only one gift. Remember, we are all given *some* kind of gift or talent to produce more income for the Lord.

The Lord gives us these gifts for the profit of all. This is done so He may get a return on His investments. The anointing is God's currency with man, and that is why in Matthew 25:18, Jesus said: *"But he that had received one went and digged in the earth, and hid his lord's money* [gift or talent]." God knows who will be good stewards or investors of His anointing. So, if we are lacking in the anointing, it's very likely we need to increase our investment skills.

We may be asking ourselves, how can we increase our investment skills? I have an answer for you. The last letter in TAP stands for *principles*. The word *principle* in Hebrew has several different meanings, such as the word *reshith*, which means beginning, chief, or first fruit. It stems from the word *rosh*, which means the head, the first in place, time, order, or rank. Another Hebrew word that defines it perfectly is the word *moetsah*, which means a purpose, counsel, plans, or devices. Principles are there to fulfill God's purposes on earth. It's also defined as plans or devices. The Lord gives us strategies to enhance our quality of life though following these principles. Principles are the counsel of God to navigate us to our divine destiny. See, God is no respecter of persons. However, He is a respecter of principles. When it comes to the anointing, just like in college, we have our majors and our minors. However, we have a lot of people majoring in their minors and minoring in their majors. We have pastors trying to be prophets and prophets trying to be pastors. This is the reason we are not receiving the fullness of God. Because we are out of position and out of rank, we lack understanding on the method of God's government.

Another meaning of *principle* is a fundamental law or truth upon which others are based—a moral standard. When something is fundamental, it is of major significance and the primary origin of everything that springs from it. Principles are significant to a believer's walk. When we follow God's principles, then we can find the *"Prince"* in the principle. The Lord shows us who He is, through His attributes. If we follow the principles outlined in this book, we can obtain every promise and possess every gift, talent, and anointing God has in store for us who are good stewards. So let's get ready to TAP!

NOTES

1. All Hebrew and Greek definitions are from *The New Strong's Complete Dictionary of Bible Words* by James Strong (Thomas Nelson, 1996).

2. English definitions are from *Webster's Pocket Dictionary and Thesaurus of the English Language*, new rev. ed. by V. Nichols (Nichols Publishing, 1999).

3. Biblical references are from *Zondervan's Compact Bible Dictionary* by T. Alton Bryant, (Zondervan, 1994), and *Smith's Bible Dictionary* by William Smith (Thomas Nelson, 1964).

Chapter 1

GLORY CHASERS

THE ANOINTING VERSUS THE GLORY: WHAT IS THE ANOINTING?

The origin of the word *anointing* was from a practice of shepherds during biblical times. Lice and other insects would often get into the wool of the sheep. These pests would get near the sheep's head and burrow to enter the sheep's ears. They infected the sheep so much they became sick and eventually die. So, the ancient shepherds poured oil on the sheep's head, making the wool slippery. This was done to make it impossible for insects to get close to the sheep's ear because they would slide right off of the oil. From this, the anointing, or the actual anointing oil I should say, became symbolic of blessing, protection, and empowerment.

The anointing of God is for a similar purpose. It is there to remove any spiritual insects of the enemy that will try to get in our ear and eventually kill us. It may not kill us physically. However, it can kill our financial harvest, our witness, our creditability as a believer in Christ, and worst of all it can kill our vision for God's purpose. If satan can get to our vision, he can destroy us. He knows *"Where there is no vision, the people perish"* (Prov. 29:18). The anointing is the access code to the glory of God. Many people think the two are different. However, we can't have one without the other. The New testament Greek word for *anoint* is the word *chrio*, which means "to anoint or consecrate with rubbing or pouring of oil." By implication, this was the process to consecrate someone for office either as a king, prophet, or to become a builder.

This also signified God's blessing or call on that person's life. The anointing is vitally important for many reasons, the main one being because it gives the believer their identity in Christ. There are multitudes of believers who know how to get in God's presence. However, once it lifts they are still lost about who they are in Him. Many backslide because they have no sense of direction in their calling for God. They don't understand their placement in church, the five-fold ministry, or their mission for God's Kingdom. This is the reason why vast numbers of people hop from church to church and meeting to meeting searching for validation of their calling.

I want to address a few misconceptions about the anointing. It has been taught that when operating under the glory, we should not lay hands because then it becomes the anointing realm not God's glory realm. This statement is very far from the truth. Laying hands does not mean we are moving under the anointing instead of the glory. Instead, it means we have transitioned to the point of contact position in God's glory. The reason many get tired when laying hands is due to the fact that they were operating in the flesh from the start. Jesus laid hands on thousands of people and never got tired. I explain this in more detail in Chapter 3 under the subtitle "Hands-on Training."

Many have wondered—was Jesus operating in the anointing or the glory when He laid hands on the people? I present the argument that the two are one and the same. According to Luke 4:18, Jesus said, "*The Spirit of the Lord* [or the glory of God] *is upon me, because he hath anointed me,*" and then He listed the things He was anointed to do. Remember, the anointing means to smear upon, rub, or pour upon. This means it comes upon us like the glory does. Therefore, yokes get destroyed because of the anointing or anointing oil (see Isa. 10:27). Without the use of the anointing, people will stay stuck in bondage. I have been to many glory gatherings and seen people experience signs and wonders and some healings. I have also seen many leave those same meetings still broken, oppressed, depressed, and unfulfilled. Someone asked me one day, "Why is this so?" I told them the people left unchanged because they experienced an atmospheric touch. However, they weren't anointed to receive an infilling that would have allowed them to remain in that realm. Once they returned to their homes, that experience that was in the meeting lifted because their atmosphere at home was totally different.

Glory realm atmospheres can lift or be hindered for various reasons. However, an impartation of the anointing remains whether it is in seed form or full measure within that individual. If someone receives the baptism of the Holy Spirit, it is in them forever. On the other hand, an atmospheric glory, as many refer to it, can be removed through hindrances in worship. It can be because the church we are ministering in does not understand that realm. It can be because the people are so used to hands being laid on them to build their faith that they have received something. It can be because they don't have patience to tarry in the glory until something manifests. In the majority of cases, the atmosphere is not conducive for the glory cloud to come in or manifest. Many churches can get a cloud to come but don't have the patience to wait for the rain. This is where the anointing kicks in.

There is no record of Jesus waiting for the atmosphere to be right before He moved in healing, deliverance, or creative miracles. Many people use the Scripture in Luke 5:17 to argue this claim because it mentions *"The power of the Lord was present to heal them,"* which is true. However, this was actually talking about the strong anointing being upon Jesus to demonstrate healing. For example, the apostle Peter was so anointed that it radiated through his body at such a far distance, until even his own shadow healed the sick. That manifestation wasn't atmospheric, because if that was the case they wouldn't have needed Peter or his shadow to receive their healing. Remember, they were living in an area where the miraculous was plentiful. However, it occurred not because of the atmosphere, but the anointing upon Peter's life created this phenomenon. The people even recognized and acknowledged that it was through his shadow that these miracles occurred (see Acts 5:15).

Jesus never waited for any opportune time to administer God's power; instead, He just stepped into the realm of the Spirit through the anointing that was upon Him, and miracles took place. Jesus was called "the Christ," which means *anointed one,* not the glory one. If we want to be like Christ, we must seek to be anointed and move in His anointing. I don't make this next statement to brag or boast. However, I move very heavily in the glory realm or the atmospheric anointing of God's presence, for a better term. What I have noticed is that most people who operate in this realm can't function in any other facet of the anointing. They are so codependent on the atmospheric flow that they can't even lay hands on a simple headache and make it go away. If we only operate in this one position of the anointing, we cripple our capabilities to do more in the spirit realm. Many in the Body of Christ have become lazy and afraid to step out to minister because they are waiting for a certain temperature in the spirit to arise.

If you notice, Jesus never waited for a worship or praise team to be there to set the atmosphere for Him to minister. Jesus was so used to engaging in a point of contact anointing until the Roman centurion had to urge Him not to get up to come to his home. However, he urged Jesus to just send His word and his servant would be healed (see Matt. 8:5-13). High faith is the principle we must put into action to operate effectively in the no point of contact realm. Jesus responded to the Roman centurion saying "I never saw such great faith in all of Israel." This type of miracle or manifestation will not take place in a conducive atmosphere. However, it will manifest in a high faith environment. Jesus never rebuked the disciples for not having enough glory or enough anointing. However, he did rebuke them for lack of faith. As we go from glory to glory, our faith must arise with each new level of glory. This is why the Scriptures say "*from faith to faith*" and "*from glory to glory*" (Rom. 1:17; 2 Cor. 3:18).

The anointing reveals our true relationship with God. The measure of power that flows through us reveals how much we've been seeking God. In the glory, there is less work and warfare. However, I have seen many people become so lazy and dependent on the glory that when it lifts, they cannot bring any form of deliverance to the captives. When we constantly depend on one facet of God, we start to lose ground in other realms of the spirit. In the glory, the Father fights for us. In the anointing, he allows us to stand up and fight for ourselves. This builds up our work ethic and endurance as soldiers in His Kingdom. With the anointing, we are more than civilians. Therefore, we need to keep a military mind-set and remind ourselves daily that we are not only sons and daughters of God—we are also soldiers in His army.

The main point is that the anointing of God is just as important as moving in the glory realm, if not more so. Many don't have the patience to wait to move in the glory or wait for the atmosphere to be conducive. However, many have accepted Jesus and received the baptism and anointing of God. We just have to stir it up, step out on faith, and the Holy Spirit will do the rest. I would like to emphasize that this topic is not intended to disrespect or discredit those who believe only in the sovereign realm of God's glory. However, this was to give the body of believers a different facet on how to minister. We are already fully equipped; we just need to look inside ourselves, and we will find ourselves and TAP!

WHAT IS THE GLORY?

I decided I wanted all the different facets of God's anointing. So, on my search I ran into this new term called the *glory realm*. I had heard of the anointing of God before but never heard of the glory realm. I began to search the Scriptures concerning the word *glory,* and I found many definitions, translations, and explanations.

What is *glory?* The word translated as "glory" in our English Bible comes from several Hebrew and Greek words with various meanings. For instance, many people are familiar with the Hebrew word *kabod,* which means "splendor," "honor," "reverence," "abundance," "weight or heaviness." The Greek word *doxa* means "renown," "praise," "opinion," or "the unspoken manifestation of God." All of these words have been translated as "glory" in various places in the Bible.

The Hebrew word *Shekinah* is not in the Bible but is used in Jewish theology to refer to the presence of God and is also found in the targumim writings. The targumim or targum writings were spoken paraphrases, explanations, and expansions of the Jewish scriptures that the rabbi would give in the common language of the listeners. *Shekinah* refers to the majestic presence of God; it means "to dwell or settle" among men. I knew that was what I needed, so the hunt was on. This was all new to me, so I had to become a student of those who moved in the glory. I had to start at the beginning and work my way up.

WHAT WAS THE DIFFERENCE?

In my journey to discover this new realm of God's anointing called the *glory realm*, I needed to first understand what the difference was between the glory realm and the anointing. Listed below are the differences that I found in my search to understand both dimensions of God's ways of demonstrating His power. Let me explain:

The Anointing

1. In the anointing it's like taking the stairs, but being in the glory is like taking the elevator. Everything accelerates in the glory.

2. In the anointing it may take time to see a result, while in the glory it's instantaneous because time is removed from the equation.

3. In the anointing I saw more healings and deliverances take place, but in the glory realm I saw more creative miracles and signs and wonders manifest.

4. In the anointing there are levels and measures, but in the glory there are dimensions and realms.

5. In the anointing there is an infilling, but in the glory there is more of an outpouring.

6. In the anointing we have to work our faith. However, in the glory we just rest and declare and decree from an open heaven.

7. In the anointing, God works with us according to Mark 16:20. But in the glory, God does the work for us through the angelic assistance from an open heaven.

Through this journey it seemed that the glory realm was much easier and required less work ethic on my part. However, as I began to operate in this newfound discovery called the glory realm, I also saw some side effects to operating in this realm alone.

The Glory

1. The glory displays how powerful God is, but the anointing shows how powerful we are in God. The anointing exposes how much we have God in us, not just around us through atmospheric help from above.

2. In the glory realm, there is rest. However, there is still a labor to enter into that rest before we can command or decree things from that realm. However, in the anointing we can just step into action through faith or the quickening of the spirit without tarrying to get an atmosphere to show up.

3. In the glory, we may get a cloud to come, but it does not guarantee rain will fall upon the people and manifestation will happen. In the anointing, we have grown accustomed to our gift, whether it's a healing anointing, the prophetic, deliverance, etc. So, we

know how to work that gift, through the unction and quickening of the Holy Spirit, to the point of guaranteed results every time. This happens because now the Holy Spirit entrusts us with this gift through the anointing and praying for people.

4. The majority of the time, the glory realm is displayed in conferences, church settings, and spiritual functions. The reason being is that we have to set an atmosphere through a worship or praise team first before administering manifestations of God's glory. When we are operating in the anointing, we can go just about anywhere and display His power in the streets, grocery stores, hair salons, etc.

My wife goes to the nail shops and salons often and people come out with makeup running down their faces and hair all out of place because she administered the anointing. People there were healed or delivered from demonic forces. She does this everywhere she goes; she is not bound because the atmosphere wasn't conducive or because she didn't have a band or radio to get her started. It's the anointing in her and upon her that makes it happen.

The anointing and the glory both have their side effects. However, they are both needed and both work together for God's purpose and plan for the people. We can't have one without the other. My biggest issue is when I see a minister discredit the anointing or downplay it like it's a weaker version of God's power. I also disagree with ministers who teach about the anointing like it is an old school version of the glory realm. In all actuality, they are both one and the same. One is atmospheric and one is through point of contact, and if we recall, Jesus moved in both. If Jesus our Lord moved in both in His earthly ministry, so should we.

INTRODUCTION INTO THE GLORY

I was in Dallas for a revival led by a pastor I knew. The pastor had guest speakers coming from out of town—Sito and Lucy Rael. I was only used to the ministers I saw on Christian television. I'd heard about this glory business for several months. I'd seen YouTube clips of people like Joshua Mills who'd witnessed manifestations of gold dust. However, I wasn't quite sure if this stuff was real or not. I wanted the glory, but I didn't really know what I was asking for.

I sat in the third row of this meeting. I watched gold dust fall from the pages of Lucy Rael's Bible. I also saw oil begin to drip from her hands. The icing on the cake was when blood started to flow out of her hand like the crucifixion of Jesus. I said to my friend, "This lady is either a witch or this is all staged."

Then, she walked down the aisles and spoke words of knowledge over the people. At first, she passed me by, but then she backtracked to me and said, *"You're God's prophet, and don't question anymore who you are."* It was confirmation of the call I'd heard all along. All of a sudden, thick gold dust appeared in my hand, and the whole crowd started taking pictures. Lucy laid hands on me, but only on my shoulder. I finally had an experience in the glory realm. Now mind you, I still was not quite sure about Sister Lucy because I had heard rumors about her being fake, and that the manifestation was all a hoax. I heard she was under T.L. Osborn's ministry at one time, even considered as one of his spiritual daughters. However, I told the Holy Spirit, "If this is not real, I still want the authenticity of this manifestation."

I believe that because of my prayer and the fact that my hunger was so strong for the glory and supernatural things of God, He honored my request. Even if we think something is from the enemy because it is strange to our theology or seemingly a hoax, we must still pray and ask for the authenticity of the manifestation. We must pray and believe that God will make His demonstration of power more potent than the enemy's. It is important to note that satan is merely a copycat of God's anointing. Moses performed miracles similar to the Egyptians magicians. However, Moses' snake was more potent than the Egyptians' snakes and sorcery. Why do we think the Lord chose the snake miracle as a sign? Well, the answer is, He was testing that spirit according to First John 4:1. See, God foreknew that the Egyptians would manifest that snake miracle as a magical sign to challenge Moses. The Lord decided to manifest His sign first, knowing He would win the competition. Elijah also challenged the prophets of Baal with the same miracle, with the intent to show whose god was greater.

The manifestation is not the issue, but it's the deity behind it that makes the difference. If a modern-day minister performs a snake miracle or a fire miracle in today's times, people will arrest him and scream he is of the devil. We as believers must stop being afraid of manifestations we don't understand. Just ask the Holy Spirit, "If this is of God, give it to me; if not, give me the original, godly version of this manifestation." It's just that simple. The only thing to really fear is making critical statements against a move of the Holy Spirit. We don't want to find ourselves blaspheming against God's Spirit because we don't understand certain things. The next time we find ourselves questioning a certain manifestation, just pray that prayer and watch God bring the true fruit forth from that encounter.

When I later returned to Houston from that meeting, heavy gold dust started manifesting at our meetings. I asked the Lord to show me a Scripture that confirmed the gold dust manifestations were from Him. He gave me Job 28:6: *"The stones of it are the place of sapphires: and it hath dust of gold."* Wow! It was right there in Scripture, even though the context was referring to wisdom. The revelation was that when we obtain the wisdom of God the gold dust will appear. Once God gave me wisdom about the manifestations, the gold just began to pour and pour. I share this wisdom with you now, so let the golden glory fall. Sister Lucy introduced me to the glory in a way I had never experienced. I knew then that the best was yet to come; I had now entered into the glory realm.

HOW TO TAP INTO THE GLORY REALM

Here are a few tips I use to TAP into the glory realm of God.

Speak of the Glory

In Psalms 145:11-12, the Scriptures tell us, *"They shall speak of the glory of thy kingdom, and talk of thy power; to make known to the sons of men his mighty acts, and the glorious majesty of his kingdom."*

To move in the glory realms we must speak of the glory of God. I have learned that the more I speak on the subject of God's glory, the more it manifests in our meetings. Whatever we address will manifest; this goes for any subject concerning God's manifestation. This is why I tell people to really ponder on what they're going to name their conferences and events; having the right name for the event will be one of the determining factors of what will manifest. When someone invites me out to a glory conference, I now know what to prepare for. It's the same when it comes to prophetic schools or conferences. I tune in my faith for that specific anointing because that's where the people's faith will be when I arrive. The Scriptures say it like this in Romans 12:6, *"Having then gifts differing according to the grace that is given to us, whether prophecy, let us prophesy according to the proportion of faith."* Wherever our faith level is, that's what will manifest when we minister to the people. I have also learned that we cannot manifest what our mind is not paying the most attention to. We cannot demonstrate what we are not willing to articulate. To *articulate* means "the ability to speak fluently and coherently on a consistent basis." If we make an effort to expound on the subject of the glory of God, it will attract His presence in our lives and saturate our atmospheres with the splendor of His majesty. We must talk His presence to existence. Closed mouths don't get fed.

Another principle key is to speak of His power daily. Daily conversations of God's power will put us in position to receive more authority from Him. Many believers think that God's glory is His power. However, this is not so. God's glory is His presence and His person. However, His power is a separate entity of God's glory. That's what we will see in Scriptures like, *"Not by might, nor by power, but by my spirit, saith the Lord"* (Zech. 4:6), or like, *"For thine is the kingdom, and the power, and the glory, for ever. Amen"* (Matt. 6:13). These verses show the difference between His glory, His power, and His Spirit. God's power in the Greek is the word *dunamis*, which means might, strength, marvelous works, and the ability to perform. God's *dunamis* power is for the purpose of growing the believer in sanctification and preparing them for heaven's glorification. His power is to help us identify with our God-like nature. This also allows them to simultaneously experience measures of that power in the earth realm.

Without God's power, we are defenseless against the wiles of the devil. It is important to confess the power of God daily, whether it was demonstrated in the Bible or in our own personal encounters. As we begin to speak on it, that realm will open up and reenact the same demonstrations of power. For example, when Elisha the student captured his master Elijah's mantle, he went to the riverbed where his teacher had once performed a miracle and he yelled, *"Where is the Lord God of Elijah?"* Then, the riverbed split just like it did before for his master (2 Kings 2:14). The student Elisha wanted to recap what his leader demonstrated before him, and the results were the same. We must revisit the demonstrations of power God has performed in His word and remind Him of those miracles. If he has done it in the past, we can experience it again in our present situation. So, the next time we are in need of an impossible miracle, we need to find a Scripture or a past memory of a miracle to demonstrate our faith with. Then we yell, *"Where is the Lord God of Elijah?"*

Fasting

Another tip to TAP into the glory is found in Isaiah 58:8: *"Then shall thy light break forth as the morning, and thine health shall spring forth speedily: and thy righteousness shall go before thee; the glory of the Lord shall be thy reward."* In the original Hebrew text, it means "Adonai's glory will follow you." Notice that the glory of God will attach itself to us when we follow this principle. The context of this Scripture was referring to the principles of fasting. Now, before you close the book and throw it on the shelf to collect dust, please hear me out. I know the subject of fasting is not the most sought after principle or practice in the Body of Christ. However, it is one of the most important principles if we want to see God's glory on earth as it is in heaven. It is one of the main secrets to our ministry's success and accomplishments.

Let me expound on the subject matter. In Isaiah 58:8, the author writes on the benefits of fasting to entice the reader's appetite for this ancient principle. The reason I use the word *appetite* is because fasting is not starving; it's actually feasting. When we engage in the principles of fasting, we are actually trading one food for another. We must transition from feasting on earthly food to feasting on the person of Jesus. John 6:55, Jesus tells us *"For my flesh is meat indeed, and my blood is drink indeed."* Jesus is the only nourishment we need during the time of fasting. John 6:55 also refers to Christ suffering His own body so we can partake in His glory.

Fasting is not suffering; instead, it is supping on God's glory. The reason fasting gets such a bad reputation is that it requires a selfless mind-set. It's for us to reject our natural appetite to satisfy God's appetite. It's a time for God the Father to feast off our prayers and praise. Next, I would like to make a statement through past experiences with all humility: "Fasting brings our answers faster." Now, most teachers on fasting will disagree with this statement and make alternative statements like, "Fasting changes your mind-set, but not God's." They make these statements to appear extra spiritual and humble. However, this is a false humility statement and unscriptural.

Throughout the entire Bible, whenever fasting was implemented God did the following:

1. God healed the lands and forgave sinful cities like Nineveh through repentance and fasting (see Jonah 3:5).

2. He saved the chosen people through Esther's fasting (see Esther 4:16).

3. Twice, He gave His word through Moses' fasting (see Exod. 24:18; 34:28).

4. Empowered Jesus for His earthly ministry when He fasted (see Luke 4:1-14).

5. He heard Daniel's prayer the first day he decided to fast (see Dan. 10:12).

Cornelius was a Gentile who supported the Jewish community through prayers and giving alms. However, one day he incorporated fasting into his routine. After which an angel appeared to him, and that occurrence itself positioned him and his entire family to become the first Gentile believers to receive the baptism of the Holy Spirit (see Acts 10:30). From the few examples in Scripture I just gave, it seems as if God had a change of heart toward a matter whenever a people would humble themselves with prayer and fasting.

I have seen stroke victims who were paralyzed on one side of their bodies get completely healed. They would run around the church brand new as a result of me doing a water fast for three days and three nights. I have witnessed blinded eyes completely open only after a five-day, all-liquid fast. In addition to these miracles, after a twenty-one-day juice and water fast I have seen many crippled people walk and tumors completely dissolve. I have even seen money materialize in people's wallets, purses, and bank accounts after I prayed. I had only fasted for a half a day during that time. You might be asking yourself, what point is he trying to make? Well, basically my point is we don't have to kill ourselves to see God move mightily through us. To be honest with you, I haven't done many forty-day fasts. The longest periods of fasting I have done consistently were a lot of twenty-one-day, water-only fasts. Then there are the three to five days of twenty-four hours around the clock dry fasting I do often, which are a killer. On those fasts, I eat no food or drink no water day and night. Those are the fasts that I put into practice the most.

I want to emphasize that we don't have to do a forty-day-water-fast to do miracles like Jesus. I have seen those kinds of miracles just on a three- or five-day fast. Forty-day fasts are powerful, don't get me wrong; I have done several myself. However, the key principle here is that successful fasting is accomplished by a consistent determination to apply it to our lifestyle, not a one-time practice. It must become a relationship ritual, not a religious routine. After reading this portion of the book, in your spare time ask the Lord to give you a specific type of fast that will be suitable for you. Also, it is important to check with your physician to make sure your body can handle certain types of fasting, especially if you are taking any prescribed medications. Once we TAP into the fasting principle, Adonai glory will follow us.

The Principle of Desire

Here is one of my favorite tips to TAP into the glory—it basically sums up this entire book. This principle I'm referring to is more of a mind-set than an actual practice. That subject I'm speaking of is the "principle of desire." Let me explain. Desire is a strong feeling of wanting to have something or wishing for something to happen. In Hebrew, "desire" is the word *avah*, which means to crave, to incline, or longing. When we are trying to get closer to God and experience His glory, a longing must take place. I have learned that whatever I want out of life, it must first be birthed out through desire before I can see results. Mark 11:24 tells us, *"Therefore I say unto you, What things soever ye desire, when ye pray, believe that ye receive them, and ye shall have them."* The main thing that sticks out here is *what things so ever we desire.* We must know God doesn't mind us desiring things. The Scripture says what things so ever we desire shall be granted. The false humility doctrine has taught us not to desire things from God—only desire God.

The reason we see no major manifestations in our day and age is because we think it's wrong to desire them. Our desire for God's blessings and manifestations does not take away from our desire to know Him. Matter of fact, it's through His blessings and manifestations that we learn of His unconditional love for us. The main reason we as modern-day believers don't see the gifts of the spirit in full operation, like the early church did, is due to the lack of desire.

First Corinthians 14:1 says *"Follow the way of love and eagerly desire gifts of the Spirit, especially prophecy"* (NIV). We must eagerly desire spiritual gifts.

I have heard many people, even anointed ministers in the faith, make unscriptural statements like "don't desire the gifts; only desire the gift giver." Even though this sounds holy and humble, it's still unscriptural. The apostle Paul was urging us to pursue these manifestations of the Holy Spirit, especially the gift of prophecy. Whatever gift we desire, that gift will eventually attract itself to us. Paul then later said in First Corinthians 14:39, *"Therefore, brethren, desire earnestly to prophesy, and do not forbid to speak with tongues"* (NKJV). Again, we see the apostle Paul prompting us to desire the gifts or manifestations of God's Spirit. We have not, because we ask not. Proverbs 11:23 says, *"The desire of the righteous is only good: but the expectation of the wicked is wrath."* If we have been made righteous in Christ Jesus our Lord, then anything we desire is considered good in His sight. The more we desire things from Him, it shows our dependence and reliance on Him as our provider. Deuteronomy 14:26 says, *"And thou shalt bestow that money for whatsoever thy soul lusteth after, for oxen, or for sheep, or for wine, or for strong drink, or for whatsoever thy soul desireth: and thou shalt eat there before the Lord thy God, and thou shalt rejoice, thou, and thine household."* This text was referring to the blessings that came with obeying the principles of tithing. I'm not here to emphasis tithing, so don't get nervous. I'm here to get us to realize how much the Lord wants us to desire material things.

When we don't desire the blessings of the Lord or even the desires of our souls, it's like a child slapping the hand of a parent who's trying to feed them. Remember, in this passage God commanded them to spend the money on themselves. When we don't enjoy the blessings, we reject the source they're coming from. The Lord wants us to delight ourselves in His provision. Psalms

37:4 says, "*Delight thyself also in the Lord: and he shall give thee the desires of thine heart*." The more we delight ourselves in the Lord, He will in turn grant us our heart's desires. This again shows us that the Lord doesn't mind us having our personal goals, dreams, and wants fulfilled. Psalms 21:1-2 says, "*The king shall joy in thy strength, O Lord; and in thy salvation how greatly shall he rejoice! Thou has given him his heart's desire, and hast not withholden the request of his lips.*" We see again that when there is a rejoicing and enjoyment in the Lord, our prayer requests and heart's desires get answered.

The problem with most believers is we don't have enough joy in our lives. We are either stressing, worrying, or depressed about certain factors in our lives that will not change until we learn to rejoice in the midst of it all. I urge everyone who is reading this part of the book to make it an urgent assignment to rejoice regardless of their circumstances. I want us to also begin to desire more things from God. Desire spiritual gifts, desire material gifts, and watch how the Lord begins to engulf us with His goodness and glory.

HOW TO BECOME A GLORY CHASER

To become a glory chaser, there are several laws or principles we must apply.

1. *A chaser must learn and study what he or she is chasing.*

Intense study of a subject will activate what we like to call the *law of attraction*. In this law, we will discover principles that inevitably lead us to our desired objective. When we, as the chaser sow seeds of interest, we will reap the attention of our target. That will then set off a chain reaction that will draw them, or it, to us.

Here is a Scripture reference: *"Draw nigh to God, and he will draw nigh to you"* (James 4:8). *Drawing* is defined as a gravitational pull or magnet that forces two counterparts to connect. I tell people all the time that every great man and woman of God I've had the privilege of coming in contact with had no choice but to encounter me. You may say, "How is that?" Well, I am a curious and inquisitive student, and that principle influenced their judgments about me and caused them to lower their guards and accept me into their circle.

You may say, "I don't want to chase after a man; I want to chase after God." Well, the same principle applies whether we are chasing after a man or God. If we're operating under the law of the student, it will cause the teacher to teach us. There is an old saying, "When the student is ready, the teacher will come." Remember, the chase is always for learning purposes, whether directly from God or from an anointed mentor. So get prepared, because the teacher is coming. The quicker we learn how to chase, the less we wait for our big break.

2. *Become a diligent seeker.*

In Hebrews 11:6, the Scripture says, *"But without faith it is impossible to please him: for he that cometh to God must believe that he is, and that he is a rewarder of them that diligently seek him."* There is a reward system for diligence, and once it's implemented the possibilities are endless. The word *diligent* is from the Greek word *spoude*, which means "prompt," "energetic," "speed." It means "striving after something" or "swiftness to show zealous actions." We must move promptly in the things of the spirit. Many believers need a thousand revelations and a million confirmations before we do the application. This is why we see little to no manifestation that we desire.

It grieves me when I hear believers say, "That's the third or fourth confirmation I've received." God has told them to start a business or write a book, but because they are waiting for another confirmation they end up forfeiting the promise that was attached to the original blessing. Now, when that person finally starts pursuing their vision, they encounter strong resistance because the anointing is no longer on that particular word of promise like before. The enemy has had time to discover the plan and protection that was on that *rhema* word. Once the devil realizes that protection has been lifted, he has access to destroy our plans and purpose. When this happens, the only solution is to bind the enemy and loose words of blessing to get the promise back. Quick obedience is the key to manifestation of the promise.

Jesus said in Matthew 12:29, "*Or else how can one enter into a strong man's house, and spoil his goods, except he first bind the strong man? and then he will spoil his house.*" A lack of diligence will force us into the role of a police officer. We must now storm the strong man's (the devil's) house, arrest (bind) him, and proceed to repossess the goods and promises he has stolen from us. Remember, the strong man is a thief and the only goods he possesses are the ones he has stolen from us. If we fail to be diligent when God gives us a blessing for seeking Him, the enemy will gain the access codes to all of our blessings and steal them right from under us without being detected.

The seeker must do more than seek to receive their reward. We must also be diligent. To be diligent, we must be energetic. That means we must be quick, prompt, and full of zeal. A person with zeal but no revelation will get further than someone with revelation and no zeal. The person with revelation thinks he has mastered that realm because of his or her obtained knowledge on the subject. That person becomes comfortable because he or she believes their revelation will seal their position in that realm. In all actuality, too much head knowledge inhibits our ability to complete a project. That's why God wants us to go back to our first love and regain the simplicity of a relationship with Him (see Rev. 2:4).

The Body of Christ has turned obtaining God into a complex process. In reality, it only requires simple faith to receive Him. Now, the person with zeal will achieve quicker results because of their persistence, which means "to continue firmly despite obstacles." The person with zeal will face more warfare because of a lack of knowledge. However, experience becomes their best teacher. Consistent victories increase their confidence and compel them to keep going from glory to glory. When we become diligent seekers of God, no devil in hell can block our blessings.

3. *Endurance*

Last but not least in the law or principle of becoming a glory chaser is the principle of endurance. In the course of our journey, we will encounter obstacles and hardships. In Second Timothy 2:3, it says: *"Thou therefore endure hardness, as a good solider of Jesus Christ"* Our endurance of hardship will determine whether we are good soldiers for the Lord or not. The modern-day believer wants the white picket fence, the big house, and no trials and troubles. People of God, this is a false hope. Once we become a born-again believer, the fight is on. Most believers want to be civilians and not soldiers. According to Webster's dictionary, the definition of a *civilian* is "a person not serving in the military, as a firefighter or as a policeman." When we're a civilian and not a solider for Christ, we can't fight the fiery darts of the enemy. When we're a civilian and not a solider, we can't bind or arrest the devil because we don't carry the authority of a spiritual police officer or military personnel. When we're a civilian and not a solider in God's army, we are basically left defenseless.

Just as boot camp builds up the muscles of a soldier, having endurance will build up our spiritual authority. The objective of boot camp or hardship is to break down the weak elements inside of an individual. This is done so that he or she may be reconfigured into a well-disciplined, combat-equipped, demon-killing machine. I don't know about you, but I refuse to have my destiny stolen from me. I am not afraid of facing my trials and hardships. I've heard stories of anointed men and women of God who didn't want to cast out demons because they retaliated against them. Jesus said in Mark 16:17, *"And these signs shall follow them that believe; In my name shall they cast out devils."* This is a command, not a choice or suggestion. If we don't manifest these signs, then we were not assigned. Let's learn to go where God tells us to go, do what He tells us to do, and we will be what He wants us to be, and that's a glory chaser.

I pray that everyone who reads this chapter and these prayers becomes a glory chaser. Father God, let their zeal line up with your will. Bless their feet as they chase the cloud of your glory. May the King of glory come in and live with them in their homes, jobs, relationships, bodies, and families in Jesus' name. Amen.

Chapter 2

MISERY INTO A MINISTRY

The story of my conversion is all facts and no fiction. It starts with tragedy but ends in triumph. It may seem raw and uncut. However, it depicts the harsh reality of the strongholds the devil has on certain parts of society today. I will give you the PG-13 version of the story to protect certain people's identities and lives. Certain information I will not omit. These statements cannot be used to reopen any criminal court cases that have been closed. That is double jeopardy, according to the law. So, let's begin.

My name is Shawn Anthony Morris. I was born in New Orleans, Louisiana on December 10, 1979 to Audrill Morris and Bill Hurst. From day one, my biological father denied that I was his. He and his mother, brothers, and sisters were well-known drug dealers and murderers in the city. My mother's side of the family was a little different, although they lived around the crime-infested Calliope

Projects. My mother grew up in a fairly decent household with both her mother and father in the home. There was one issue—my grandparents had six kids, but my mother was the only one who was dark-skinned, besides my uncle Percy. The rest of her siblings were light-skinned with blue or green eyes and looked Caucasian.

My mother's family was mixed with Jewish, French, Indian, and African heritages. My father's side was Native American, Irish, Italian, and African. Because of my mother's dark complexion, her siblings teased her and insisted that she was adopted. She was the literal black sheep of the family. So, my mother grew up bitter, and she was plagued by a spirit of rejection that opened her up to a manic-depressive spirit later in life.

MY BIRTH

I was born prematurely with a hole in my heart, and the doctors thought I wasn't going to make it. But I did! The devil tries to kill many prophets at birth because he has a glimpse of their future and destiny. He tries his best to abort the blessing before it's fully developed. He tried to kill Moses at birth (see Exod. 1:16), as well as our Messiah Jesus Christ (see Matt. 2:16-18). When I was two years old, one of my mother's boyfriends tried to burn me with acid because my mother refused to be with him. Then she met my stepfather, Reginald Thompson, who was six feet three inches tall and two hundred plus pounds. He ran the other guy off. Not long after that, my mother married Reginald.

When I was born, my biological father denied me and neglected his responsibilities. My mother grew bitter toward him and eventually took it out on me. Because my biological father rejected me as his child, the spirit of rejection and depression took a toll on my mother all the more. She began to abuse me physically by burning me with cigarettes or beating me with any object she could find. Every time she would look at me, she reminded me that I looked like my father. She would humiliate me in front of my siblings and relatives; the insults would be considered as jokes. So, I grew up as the black sheep of the family, just as she did. That verbal abuse lasted throughout my childhood and adulthood.

THE SAGA BEGINS

Marrying Reginald gave my mother a brief form of acceptance, a way to escape her childhood of rejection and the hardship of raising a child on her own. My deadbeat father denied a child (me) who looked just like him. They took him to court for child support once; the judge was going to lock him up for denying me because I looked so much like him. I had no father figure or male role model to look up to. I only had the guys on the streets and my stepfather to fill that void. However, there was a little secret that my mother's husband was hiding. He was addicted to crack cocaine, a drug that hit America's inner cities like an unstoppable plague. I had no chances growing up. I had a manic-depressive mother who popped pills from time to time to escape reality. I also had an imprisoned crack dealer for a father and a crack addict for a stepfather. So basically, the streets raised me. The neighborhood dope man was my big brother, and I was my own father.

THE SAGA CONTINUES

I picked up a few bad habits and generational curses from growing up in such a hostile environment. At age eleven, I started using marijuana and alcohol, which opened the door to more demonic addictions. At the age of fourteen, I started using cocaine and then quickly developed a heroin addiction at the age of sixteen. Heroin is one of the most addictive drugs out there, even more addictive than crack cocaine. Like any powerful stronghold, if someone tries to quit cold turkey it will cause dramatic effects both mentally and physically.

Through my teenage years, I developed a criminal lifestyle. I stole cars, I robbed people, and I broke into their homes. I had shoot-outs with rival gangs and developed the reputation of a person you didn't want to mess with. I was arrested many times, once for battery on a police officer. I was facing five years in prison for that charge because I had broken the officer's arm and his jaw when he tried to apprehend me. But, by the grace of God, those charges were dropped. Once the police realized I assaulted one of their own, I was a target. That night I was arrested, they beat me up pretty badly. The doctors wrote something in the report that kind of helped me with my case. My mother put up the house for my bond, and even though I wasn't saved I knew God had something to do with it. The mercy of God was on my life even in my sinful state.

My first supernatural encounter occurred when I was fourteen. I was going to Mississippi for a family reunion. Before I left, a friend of mine told me I needed to slow down. He was referring to my habit of stealing cars and performing robberies. While in Mississippi, I met up with my cousins. We stole our relative's car and went for a joy ride. All of a sudden, we turned onto a red dirt road where this twenty- to thirty-foot ravine was. The car sped out of control and off into the air we went. As we were in the air, everything went into slow motion. The car finally landed on the ground, bounced several times, and hit a tree that split the hood of the car in half. My face went through the windshield. Glass sliced my eyelids in two, ripped flesh from my face, and cut my neck. After the collision, my face print was left on the windshield with a pair of bloody angel wings around it.

When they pulled the car out of the wreckage, it frightened everyone who saw it. What made it even stranger was the fact that I was the only one that got hurt in the car; everyone else left without a scratch. The doctors said that if I had turned my head slightly to the left or right when I went through the glass, my head would have been completely cut off. Everyone said it was a miracle that we lived through such a wreck. However, all I could think of were the bloody angel wings with my face print. That was the first supernatural encounter that I can remember; I knew from that accident that God was with me.

A few years later when I was in my twenties, I was facing ninety-nine years in prison for armed robbery and aggravated assault with a deadly weapon. They wanted to give me an attempted murder charge, which carried a heavier sentence. When I was booked, that was the charge given. I'd been involved in a shoot-out with a guy over money. The event had even made the newspapers. I was about to lose everything, and my life was about to be over.

MY PRISON ENCOUNTER

When most people get locked up in prison, one of two things takes place—they either get into more trouble or find God. I didn't know anything about God, but I knew about church. My mother made me go to a traditional Baptist church when I was growing up. Each time I went to church, I automatically fell asleep. To this day, I don't believe it was the devil that made me do that. I believe it was God's way of keeping my spirit man from feeding on and digesting religious spirits.

While in prison, I met some guys who knew about Jesus. They would sing hymns and had a joy about them even in the midst of their terrible situations. I had a choice to make—I could sit miserable in prison for the rest of my life, or I could find joy in the midst of my sorrow. So, I started attending their prayer meetings. I accepted Jesus as my Savior, and my heroin addiction left me instantly. I suffered no withdrawal symptoms; it was like I was brand new.

I vowed to God that if He got me out of prison, I would never touch heroin again. Instead, I would be fully devoted to serving Him. Well, God is a covenant keeper, and He got me out of prison. They let me go because there were no witnesses and the defendant didn't even show up to testify. The arrest record I had, there was no way they were supposed to let me go that easy. My mother thought it was because of a letter she had sent to the judge. However, it was actually my petition to the Judge who lives up above that did it. Thank you, Jesus, for setting me free.

BREACH OF CONTRACT

When I was released from prison, the first thing I did was kiss the ground and shout, "I am free!" Well, at least I thought I was. I was clean from drugs, but I still had old soul ties to my street family and neighborhood. I distanced myself from my friends for a season so I could remain on the right track and stay off drugs. However, I ended up developing a new habit—my music career.

A friend from the neighborhood I knew was a straight-up guy. He and I started a record company called "Kings of the Round Table." It was a success. We were well known locally in the New Orleans underground circle. However, we had no national status. By that time, I had three kids and a wife. I had already wasted many years pursuing aspirations of being the biggest kingpin gangster who ever lived. Now, I had once again put my family on the back burner, and this time it was to pursue a music career. In spite of their cries, I remained diligent in my chase for the American dream.

Just as I had found God in prison, I also left Him in there. The lifestyle I was leading could not coexist with His plan and purpose for my life. It's hard being an angel when you're surrounded by devils. I went back to smuggling drugs, and in my own twisted imagination I figured as long as I wasn't using them I was fine. My music became my new addiction, and I wasn't going to let anyone stop my dream. I was determined.

THE STORM AFTER MY STORMS

In August 2005, Hurricane Katrina hit the Gulf Coast of Louisiana. It was a category five storm with winds up to 175 miles per hour. It breached the levies of the Crescent City. Gas prices skyrocketed and haven't really come down since. This storm damaged a lot of oil rigs in the gulf, and homes were under water. Hundreds died in the flood, and many more died because of the late response of our government. Many women and children died because of dehydration and lack of food.

Many saw Hurricane Katrina as a catastrophic disaster of biblical proportions, and it was. It was God's judgment on a wicked city. Before the storm, the city of New Orleans had the highest murder rate in the United States. We had more murders than big cities like Los Angeles, Detroit, Chicago, and New York. A lot of people call Las Vegas Sin City. However, Las Vegas was like a safe suburb theme park compared to New Orleans, a.k.a. "The Big Easy." With its demonic heritage of voodoo possession, the French Connection drug trade, mafia controlled businesses, riverboat gambling, and one the most crooked judicial system in the United States, it was indeed

Sin City. It also served as the first city where the Sicilian Mafia landed in America. They were called "the black hand." Before they started the five families in New York and Chicago, it all started here first in New Orleans.

While others saw this storm as a tragedy, I saw it as an escape from Egypt. The pharaoh of this land was the economic and criminal justice system. It kept the people in bondage. Before Hurricane Katrina, studies showed that 85 percent of all African American males in the Orleans parish district would have been incarcerated more than fifteen times and possibly murdered before their twenty-first year of age. Where there is high poverty and low quality education, criminal activity will be high as well. So, chances of making it out of that type of environment as an African American male were slim to none. I was a perfect candidate for those statistics. Something had to change.

TO THE PROMISED LAND

Many people from Louisiana migrated to Texas after the hurricane, mostly to the Houston and Dallas areas. During the storm, I got separated from my ex-wife and my music business partner. I escaped the storm and went with my mother and children to Baton Rouge. By then, I was able to get in touch with my partner in the music business. He had fled to Houston and told me how we could make some money with the music and other vices out there. Although I was no longer on drugs, I still had a drug-dealing mentality. So, once again I left my children to chase after a dream. When I went to Houston, it seemed like a gold mine. The women seemed more appealing, the drug dealers looked more laid back and less confrontational, and I was a predator on the prowl. I thought I had hit the jackpot. However, I was in for a big surprise.

THE GAME IS NOT THE SAME

Several drug dealers from New Orleans came to Houston with the same mentality they had in the Big Easy. That mentality was, "If you don't give it, we will take it." However, Houston had a rude awakening for those people. The drug dealers in Houston had already heard of the New Orleans people's reputation for murdering and robbery. They had already prepared themselves for any backlash that may come with the two cities merging. Because of this, a lot of conflicts arose. The drug dealers from Houston refused to cut the dealers from New Orleans in on the drug trade, so the war began. The media started to refer to New Orleans evacuees as "refugees," like we were from a different country or from a faraway land. This fueled the anger of a lot of New Orleans natives. We were being profiled as animals, not just from a certain race. We also received insults from other minority groups. To be honest with you, who could blame them? The majority of the inner city youth from New Orleans had that destructive mentality that was detrimental to society.

The murder rate increased in Houston, and violence broke out in the schools among the kids from New Orleans and the kids from Houston. Houston drug dealers committed crimes knowing that the police department would blame the evacuees from New Orleans. It was a disaster, and I was in the middle of it. It seemed like the "promised land" wasn't as promising as I had thought. That spirit of murder, drug selling, and other vices had followed me from New Orleans. I had left the land of Egypt, but it seemed like the Egyptian mentality wouldn't let my people go. I was still a slave to my own self-afflicted bondage. I needed to get free.

MY CONVERSION

What is a conversion? The word *conversion* means "the act or state of changing to adopt new opinions or beliefs." In Houston, I had started a prostitution ring, making women sell their bodies for money. I was also selling drugs on the side to pay rent and to keep my music company afloat. My friend Joel was doing similar things. After a while, he and I had a falling out and parted ways. My music dreams were put on hold because he and I were going in different directions. However, Joel kept pursuing the music career without me.

I was focused on finding a way to come up and take over Houston. I had all the women, cars, drugs, and guns that I wanted. However, I still felt empty on the inside. I lost the relationship I once had with my kids in New Orleans. I was separated from my ex-wife at this time. I had really hit rock bottom, and I was only surviving off temporary satisfactions. I was on the verge of a volatile meltdown and I didn't even know it. I needed invention and I needed it quickly.

A New Friend

Before the storm came along, Joel and I were really close friends. Before our friendship begin to fade, we sold drugs together, robbed together, and made music together. Losing my friendship with him was a big blow to me. I had always thought that if there was anyone who would have my back, it would be Joel. Now, with him out of the picture, I trusted no one and my heart grew colder by the day.

One day, I heard a knock on my front door. To my surprise, it was Joel. Part of me wanted to literally shoot him. However, I still had love for him as a brother. This time something was different about him. He told me he'd gotten saved and that he was turning his life around. I had an encounter with God before in jail, but most people do. When they get out it's like that encounter never happened. However, something was different about Joel's conversion. He was humble and his face looked brighter. He even talked in a softer tone. That wasn't Joel at all! I had a "new" friend.

The Power of the Word

Joel walked into my house as a new man. I had heard all this Jesus stuff before from church people, my ex-wife, and others. To be quite frank with you, I didn't want to hear it again. I felt like I had breached my contract with God and I would just mess up again. Plus, I was entrenched so deeply in sin, how could I change? I was convinced that God couldn't forgive a murderer, pimp, drug dealer, and thief like me.

As Joel talked, he didn't preach to me about my sins. The Holy Spirit knew I would judge Joel for his past and not receive Him because of it. So, He did something very wise. The Holy Spirit told Joel to have me read Second Timothy 3:1-7 out loud:

> *This know also, that in the last days perilous times shall come. For men shall be lovers of their own selves, covetous, boasters, proud, blasphemers, disobedient to parents, unthankful, unholy, without natural affection, trucebreakers, false accusers, incontinent, fierce, despisers of those that are good, traitors, heady, high-minded, lovers of pleasures more than lovers of God; having a form of godliness, but denying the power thereof: from such turn away. For of this sort are they which creep into houses, and lead captive silly women laden with sins, led away with divers lusts, ever learning, and never able to come to the knowledge of the truth.*

Then Joel said, "Now tell me, where you find yourself in that Scripture?"

All of a sudden, a heavy feeling of conviction fell over me. I begin to weep and said, "I can't find anything in that Scripture that doesn't describe me." I found myself in the entire chapter. Then, I fell on my knees and felt an electricity travel all over my body. I cried for hours on the floor and gave my life over to Jesus Christ. I was done. I started giving away my cars and jewelry. I told the women I was pimping that I quit the business. I flushed all the drugs I had down the toilet that I was selling. The leftover addictions from other drugs like marijuana and ecstasy left me as well.

I had done everything possible to succeed in life, but all those ventures had failed. When I was finally "arrested" by the Holy Spirit. I knew I was going to be a prisoner of Christ forever. I was free, but now under a new and better yoke. This was different from my prison experience. In prison, I just wanted freedom so I could go back to the streets. Now, I just wanted freedom from sin. I was really born again.

After my conversion, many people at my job and apartment complex were also saved and delivered. We would pray for people and instant conviction would fall upon them. The managers at my job were afraid to write me up when I was late for work. They believed God would get them if they did. People were instantly filled with the Holy Spirit, and they spoke in tongues. It was glorious; people in my apartment building referred to it as the Westridge Revival. I had finally discovered the most important piece in the puzzle of life. Thank you, Jesus, for saving my soul.

On March 3, 2008, Shawn Anthony Morris was reborn!

I pray in the name of Jesus Christ that every person who reads this testimony will be born again, set free, and delivered! Lord, according to Revelation 12:11, "And they overcame him by the blood of the Lamb, and by the word of their testimony; and they loved not their lives unto the death," in Jesus' name I pray that every overcomer who speaks his or her testimony receives power from on high to destroy the enemy's camp and receive recompense for everything that was stolen from him or her. In Jesus' mighty name, it is done.

BENNY HINN ENCOUNTER

When I first got saved, all I wanted people to do was repent. I didn't have a church home or a pastor, so Joel and I started our own Bible studies in our apartment complex. We would watch TBN or Daystar Christian programs on television and listen to well-known preachers for information. However, we had no revelation about how to do what they were doing.

We were particularly drawn to Benny Hinn. At first, I thought his anointing was fake. However, for some reason I still wanted what he had. I read several of his books. The one that helped me the most was *Good Morning, Holy Spirit*. I knew my life would be different if I could encounter the Holy Spirit like Pastor Benny.

I first encountered Pastor Benny in the spirit through a night vision. In my dream, Pastor Benny and I were in a boat floating down a creek. To my left, I saw the church I was attending at the time. The land was beautiful, and the church I attended looked like the White House in Washington, DC. I saw the church members, and they were gesturing for me to come join them. All of a sudden, Pastor Benny screamed at me with a stern voice, *"Don't you listen to those people! You will build God's church in the water."* Then I woke up.

At first I was puzzled by my dream. Later on, the Holy Spirit explained to me that the church I was attending had its foundation on the land, which was built on the emphasis of the Word and faith alone and that's what the pretty green grass represented. He said my ministry would be built on the emphasis of the Holy Spirit, which is what the water represented. It was not to say that my church was wrong or not anointed. However, it was letting me know that my ministry grace would be different from theirs. That dream has come to pass, and I know it was God who sent the initial warning to me through Pastor Benny.

The Second Encounter with Pastor Benny

Joel called me one day and said, "Bro! Benny Hinn is in town!"

I asked, "Where?" He told me he was going to be at Saint Agnes' Church in Houston. So, I told Joel that I would go.

When we arrived, the church was packed with five thousand people in two different buildings. Unfortunately, our seats were in the second building, and we watched a livestream of the event happening in the main building. All of a sudden, my ex-wife started getting sleepy and sick. I didn't want to leave, even though my only choice was to watch Benny Hinn on a screen.

Several hours passed, and I started to grow weary as well. Yet, something kept telling me to stay in spite of my ex-wife's pleas to go home. Then, it was announced that Benny Hinn was coming to the second building where we were. The crowd went crazy. When he came in, it was still too packed to get to the front where he was.

Then Benny said, "I want all ministers and pastors to come to the front." I was trying to be a good husband and stay with my ailing wife, so I didn't go. All of a sudden I heard a voice say, "*Go! Now!*" So, I went forward, but the crowd was still too big for me to reach the front.

Then I heard Benny say, "You! Come here!" Everyone looked around, and so did I. He was pointing directly at me, at that point my heart began to race. I had prayed for this, for months. I had no idea what was about to take place. Time slowed down, and everything from that point progressed in slow motion. I didn't know what was about to happen. One thing I did know for sure—this was a Kairos moment being written in the heavens.

Benny Hinn Prophecy

Once I was on stage, Benny looked at me and waved his hand. All of a sudden, I felt like a strong wind had hit me, and my legs became weak. I hit the floor and began to weep uncontrollably. Just to let you know, I don't do courtesy falls for anyone, not even Benny Hinn. If I don't fall, I just don't fall. Remember, I was still a skeptic about this whole falling out in the spirit thing from the beginning. Then I heard him call someone to come on stage to pick me up. When I looked up, Joel was standing over me. Benny had called him out of a crowd of about three thousand to come and pick me up. Out of excitement Joel kept saying, "Dog! Benny Hinn! Dog! Benny Hinn!"

They picked me up, then Benny waved his hand again, and I hit the floor for the second time. He then stood over me and said, "This man has a great anointing on his life, let me tell you, he will do what I do." I couldn't believe what he had just said. Someone like me to do what Benny Hinn does? No way! I was happy with just meeting him and experiencing what I later learned was getting slain in the spirit. When I got up, I felt different but still didn't understand the full concept of it. I had received many prophecies in the past. However, this was different. It wasn't because it was Benny Hinn, it was due to the fact that I felt a tangible touch. My wife at the time didn't want to admit it, but she knew from that day forward that I was chosen by God to do great exploits for His Kingdom.

DID I REALLY RECEIVE?

A couple of days went by, and the excitement started to wane. I wondered if I had actually received something or if Benny had just spoken encouraging words to me. One thing I knew for sure was that I experienced being slain in the spirit. Replicating what Benny said seemed a little far out there. There was no way I could do what he did. I couldn't understand it at all. So, I began to go into deep prayer about it. I closed my eyes tight, and I started to pray until I felt relaxed. I started to feel light. I raised my hands to my face, and to my shock both of my hands were engulfed in blue flames. I was alarmed, but not afraid. I knew it was from God. This wasn't just a vision—flames that I could see with my natural eyes were actually on my hands. The flames were an electric blue color, like lightning but brighter. I didn't know what was taking place, but it was heavenly. That was my first time seeing in the spirit realm, and it was amazing.

As I looked, the blue flames on my hands disappeared. But something unusual was still there. My hands were hot, and I mean burning hot, but not enough to hurt me. Several days later, I asked people at my church what was going on with my hands. However, no one had an answer. I thought I might have had arthritis or carpal tunnel syndrome. I didn't know what to do.

One day I ran into a pastor and told him what had happened with Benny Hinn and the blue flames on my hands. He told me, "Brother Shawn, God has given you the healing anointing." He let me know that people like William Branham, Oral Roberts, A.A. Allen, and John G. Lake felt burning sensations in their hands when they ministered under this healing anointing. From that point on I understood what I had received. I had the explanation of the impartation to TAP and receive a gift, talent, or anointing. I now desire the same for you. So, let's continue TAPping.

IMPARTATION BUT NO ACTIVATION

I had just received this wonderful gift from the man of God. When I told people, they would tell me that God gets all the credit, man does not get any glory. I understood God gets the glory. However, I still wondered why I hadn't received this gift until the man of God laid hands on me. Then I saw in the Scriptures, *"Do not neglect the gift that is in you, which was given to you by prophecy, with the laying on of the hands of the eldership"* (1 Tim. 4:14 NKJV). That's what Pastor Benny did with me; he prophesied and then laid his hands on me as an elder in the faith. It wasn't until a man laid hands that the gift was released to me. Before this impartation from Pastor Benny, I had no knowledge of or experience with the gifts of the spirit. However, just like the Scripture says, I should not neglect the gift. To neglect something means to ignore it or fail to perform it. I was in a church that didn't allow me to operate in those gifts unless I was either commissioned by the pastors or the bishop or properly ordained. In other words, I had to go through the proper protocol. Unfortunately, to follow the protocol of my church I had to neglect my gift. I had received impartation but had no place or no one to help me activate it.

FAITHFUL BUT DYING

I was faithful to my church and my pastor. He was a real man of God. He taught me the moral standards I needed to be a real man, as well as a man of God. However, my desire for more of the

Holy Spirit was eating me alive. The women in the church had the baptism of the Holy Spirit and spoke in tongues. However, the men in the church didn't speak in tongues, not even my pastor. I knew this was not God's best. I told the Lord that He might as well have kept me in the world than have me suffer like this while trying to serve Him. I said to Him, "I want your best or nothing at all."

My church family urged me to be patient and stay humble. However, it's hard to stay patient when you're hungry for more of God. So, I asked the Lord to let my zeal line up with His will. The church had a "Minister in Training" class that I took up. However, I saw no demonstration of God's power like I had seen with Benny Hinn or like I read in Scripture about Jesus. At that time, the biggest demonstration of the Spirit that flowed through my church was prophecy, and that seemed elementary to me, even though I never did it myself.

I was at war between my faithfulness to the church and my obedience to God. Something had to give because I was dying on the vine. Many believers are more obligated to their church than they are to God's assignment for their lives. The man-pleasing spirit and fear of man's disapproval has kept many from speaking God's truth and moving to the next level in their walk. We must not be limited to man's opinion. However, we must obtain God's unlimited supply of favor for our obedience to Him. It should not be based on our obedience to man's rules. Please don't misunderstand me—I do believe in mentorship and having spiritual accountability, as long as that accountability is hearing from God and not driven by their flesh and self-made ambitions. Once I realize that leader is hearing from God for my life, then I am in total submission to their authority.

EXITING THE CHURCH AND
ENTERING THE KINGDOM

It had been a few weeks since I heard that voice at the Pastor Benny Hinn meeting. So, one day I was going to work, and that same voice said, *"Full-time ministry."*

I said to myself, "I know that is not God." I was barely able to pay the rent. I was working with my pastor on a FedEx truck delivering packages. I also worked at Popeye's as a cook. So, I told the voice, "If this is really you, God, show me!"

And the voice responded, *"I will."*

That Monday I got on the truck with my pastor as usual to make deliveries. He told me that FedEx was conducting deep background checks on all employees, including helpers. Because of my criminal record, the pastor was going to have to let me go. I was devastated. How was I going to face my ex-wife and tell her I was going to have to depend on Popeye's as my main source of income? But she didn't care. She told me she was leaving me as soon as she received her income tax return. Once again, I was devastated. I didn't know what to do or where to go. Everyone I knew was in New Orleans. I didn't want to return there because I knew God had called me to Houston.

I tried to get the pastor to give us martial counseling sessions, but my ex-wife told him she didn't want to be with me anymore. The physical and verbal abuse between my ex-wife and I became so unbearable that I resorted to sleeping in my van and taking showers at the gym where I had a membership. The pastor tried his best to keep it a secret because we both had leadership positions in the church. However, one day my ex-wife stole the van from me while I was on a job interview. I had to walk several miles to the church to get my van. I stormed into the church in a rage, and my ex-wife and

I began to physically fight in the pastor's office before service. The whole church heard the altercation. When the fight was broken up, my ex-wife gave me an evil smile and whispered, "I got you." She'd set me up for embarrassment in front of the pastor and his wife. I was humiliated. I knew my reputation in the church would only diminish from that day forward. My time was up.

It seemed as if things couldn't get any worse. I was going to work at Popeye's when the voice showed up again and said, "*I told you full-time ministry.*"

Again I said, "Show me!"

Again, the voice replied, "*I will.*"

As soon as I entered my workplace that evening, I discovered that my name was missing from the weekly schedule. They told me they were training new employees from another store and would call me if they needed me. So I said, "Okay! I got it now!"

Joel told me, "Why don't you sell your Christian rap songs on the streets to pay your bills?"

I responded, "Amen! That is a good idea!" So I pressed up fifty CDs and announced to my pastor and the church that I was going into full-time ministry. There was silence in the sanctuary.

The pastor looked up at the congregation and said, "I know some of y'all don't understand what the brother is doing. However, we're going to support him anyway. One day you might see him here, and the next day on TV somewhere." Without realizing it, the pastor was prophesying my exit out of the church and my entrance into the Kingdom. God equips us for the work of ministry, not the work of the church (see Eph. 4:12). I felt I was being pulled further and further away from the church. Even my pastor, whom I looked up to as a mentor and spiritual father, seemed distant to me as well because I refused to give up on the vision God was giving me and solely focus on the vision of the church. I then became an outcast, a rebel without a cause in the eyes of the other members of the congregation.

This succession of events made me give up on convincing the church that I was loyal. I thought I would have gained more support from my church concerning my full-time ministry decision, but I didn't. It seemed as if they took my ex-wife's side more than mine. I thought it was due to the fact that she had been with them longer. I was just a newly converted husband, so what did I know? The pastors knew of her quick temper but excused it with Scripture, saying she was a weaker vessel. Basically, they told me I should have been able to take the abuse because I am a man. As the man, if anything went wrong in my marriage, finances, kids, etc. it was due to my lack of leadership. This was a tough pill to swallow because it takes both parties to make it right or wrong. However, the verbal abuse was just as bad as the physical abuse. I knew the latest incident at the church was the last straw. I was finished. It was time to exit Egypt for the second time. Again, I would like to say it wasn't so much my pastor and his wife who were the problem. It was mainly the looks and whispers from the congregation of believers in the church that pushed me away. I loved my pastor and his wife; they were like family to me, and they still are. However, at that time God was drawing me to the wilderness to learn directly from Him.

THIS IS MY VOICE

There was a Wal-Mart across the street from the apartment complex where my ex-wife and I lived. She was so sick of my presence that she would walk into the other room when I came inside. She showed no signs of moving out, despite constantly telling me that she was leaving me. At the time, she was the only one working because I had just lost both jobs. So, I decided to go into full-time ministry. This was a language the church and she did not understand. The only one qualified for full-time ministry was the pastor, in the people's sight. However, the pastor hadn't yet stepped out in faith to make that move himself. So who was I to make such a bold statement? I wasn't the pastor, nor was I even an ordained minister. In the minds of the congregation, only the pastor had that type of faith and reason for full-time ministry. Many thought I was just using an excuse not to work. I just knew what God had told me, and it didn't matter what anyone else said. My ex-wife kept stressing that she wanted me gone. I knew it wouldn't be long before she kicked me out of the house again. So, to pay my bills I decided to sell my Gospel rap CDs in front of the Wal-Mart across the street. I was not a very good street salesman. One day I had made only three dollars in CD sales. Then that voice came to me again and said, "*Go to the bathroom and pray.*" So I walked into the store and went to the restroom to pray.

All of a sudden, a guy walked in and that voice said, "*Pray for James.*"

So I turned to the guy and said, "Sir, I know you don't know me. But God just told me to pray for James."

He looked at me with a surprised expression on his face and replied, "James? I am James."

Then cold chills rushed through my body. I told him everything about his life and family. He fell on his knees in the bathroom and gave his life to Jesus. We both walked out of the restroom crying. People gave us weird looks. After all, we were two grown men coming out of the bathroom weeping. It was the Holy Spirit who had told me to pray for James. If I had not obeyed and opened my mouth, James would not have received salvation that day. The voice that I now know to be the Holy Spirit said, "*From now on, when you hear this voice, you know this is me speaking to you.*" At that point, I knew God was with me definitely. I now had confirmation of the prophetic calling that God placed upon my life. I had finally TAPped.

A VISITATION FOR THE NATIONS

It was wintertime and I was now sleeping from house to house. One night, I had an encounter. It wasn't a mere dream; it was a visitation. I was in front of a hospital and I had two suitcases with me. So, I took my suitcases and stood in front of a bus stop. This huge bus that looked like a Greyhound bus pulled up. I got on and realized I was the only one on the bus. I was afraid because I had seen something like this in a horror movie before. I yelled out to the bus driver, "Where are you taking me?"

When the bus driver turned around and took off his hat, he had a crown of thorns on his head. I saw his eyes and blood streaming down his face. It was Jesus!

When I woke up, I was pale as a ghost. I am a dark-skinned guy, but I was as white as snow at that moment.

When I told people about my visitation, they would get goosebumps all over and become drunk in the spirit. In the week following the visitation, I went to a prophetic church and stood in line for prayer. The pastor prayed for everyone. When he came to me, he paused and looked at me. He said, "He is giving you His eyes."

Immediately the encounter flashed before my eyes, and I was slain in the spirit. I asked a few people who knew how to interpret dreams and visions; this was their interpretation. The hospital I was in front of represented the church because it's full of sick people. The suitcases indicated I was about to travel. The bus represented the size of my ministry. The part about showing me His eyes was to let me know what kind of ministry I would have. The eyes represented the seer and the prophetic anointing. The blood dripping was to let me know that I needed to live a sacrificial lifestyle. This was also an indication that I would suffer for His name's sake in order to receive and maintain that anointing.

That prophecy in the vision has come to pass. I now travel across the world preaching, prophesying, and laying hands on the sick and they recover with signs following. Imagine if I wouldn't have stepped out in faith to chase after the glory of God. I wouldn't be writing to you today. Follow the Lord, people of God, listen to His voice over the voices of the flesh, and TAP.

DISCOVERING MY DESTINY

The misery to ministry saga was coming to an end. By this time, my ex-wife and I both decided that we were finished. The love was no longer there, we were too abusive to one another. We only stayed together that long only because of ministry, not because of marriage. It was a very toxic and unhealthy relationship, so we decided it was best to part ways. I thank God for her prayers that ushered me into the Kingdom of God. It was her prayers through the years when I wasn't saved that allowed the Holy Spirit to pull me in for such a time as this. I will be forever grateful to her for that. The Lord has her Boaz who's assigned to her, and I know she will do great things for the Kingdom. Now back to the story—once the decision was made for us to part ways, I became homeless. I didn't have a job and I couldn't afford an apartment—full-time ministry wasn't generating enough income. I slept at the homes of several of my ministry friends. Being a man of God who was going through a divorce was not a popular mark to have in the church world.

The woman at the well got divorced five times. She saw Jesus and helped usher in a revival in her city. So, I had to forgive myself and not worry about the judgment of other people. If God could forgive the woman at the well for five divorces, He could forgive me for my one. I have committed other sins in my lifetime that He could have condemned me for, but He didn't. At that time in my life when everyone else wanted to stone me, He picked me up and forgave me. He then put me in a position to do His will, without the weight of guilt on my back. I thank God for being a God of second chances. However, man was not so forgiving; the warm welcomes I received were short-lived because of my situation. Even though it was our decision, I received the bulk of the blame. She received consoling for her loss. However, I left knowing that I tried my best to make it work. I was vulnerable without a wife, job, place to live, or family in Texas. I had hit rock bottom.

It was 2010. I told the Lord that if He allowed me to prophesy that the New Orleans Saints football team would go to the Super Bowl (and they did go and took home the title), then I could also prophesy my future. I was young in the faith and no one would ordain me. I wasn't looking to start a church. However, the people who came to my little revival meetings wanted my leadership. So, I decided I needed the proper licensing and credentials to pastor a church. I was young in the faith and lacked affiliation with a clergy and proper mentorship. Many pastors refused to ordain me even though they saw God working through me. So, I asked these bishops I knew to ordain me as a pastor; in turn, they told me I needed to be seasoned. However, one day God came to the bishops in their dreams. He told them to ordain the prophet (me) as a pastor in the five-fold ministry. It is important to note that when we have a purpose in life, nothing can forfeit our success. Never accept *no* as an answer when a *yes* is around the corner. I had finally found a way to TAP into my destiny. Now it was time to teach others to do the same.

I finally started to understand my journey. I knew God had a plan for my life, and His existence was more real than anything I could have imagined.

One day Reinhard Bonnke, a healing evangelist from Africa, had an impartation service in the United States. He was scheduled to be in Houston for a three-day event. My new wife, Tora, and I decided to go as we had no personal mentor at the time. We decided we were going to get all we could from God, by any means. We had adopted a baby boy named Isaiah whose mother was incarcerated. The child had two small tumors, one on his eye and one under his tongue the size of a nickel. Isaiah was only several weeks old when he was due for surgery to remove the tumors. Before the meeting, my wife turned to me and said, "Baby, I believe if you pray for him he will be healed."

I agreed. I took baby Isaiah and lifted him up in the air, proclaimed his healing, and blew on him. The baby began to throw up. Fifteen minutes later as we were leaving for the meeting, we checked the baby and the tumor on his eye was gone. It had totally disappeared, but the one under his tongue was still there. I told my wife as we walked out the door, "Don't worry. When we come back, the other one will be gone as well."

We finally arrived at the service; it was packed with more than several hundred people. We had the privilege of sitting in the pastors' section of the meeting. To my surprise, in came a wheelchair-bound Korean pastor being rolled in by his wife. They sat next to us. Several African pastors tried to pray for him, but to no avail.

All of a sudden, I heard the voice of God say, "*Pull him out of the chair.*" I did my best to ignore His voice. I began to reason with the Lord, explaining to Him how I hadn't been fasting and praying that much.

The Lord politely repeated again, *"Pull him out of the chair."*

So, I decided to ask the pastor's wife if I could pray for her husband, hoping she would say no. She agreed to allow me to pray for him, so I began to lift him out the wheelchair. His wife suddenly said, "What are you doing?"

I told her, "Just trust me," so I begin to walk with the pastor, holding him by his waist for support.

Then I heard the Holy Spirit say, *"Let him go,"* so I did. At first his legs wobbled, then all of a sudden he started to walk on his own.

The crowd went crazy. The event security guards rushed me because of the pandemonium. They said, "What are you doing?"

I replied, "I am just doing what Reinhard would do."

Then the event host said, "Let him go, and let him pray for the people."

As I prayed, people were touched by God. It was glorious. Afterward, people came up to Tora and me and asked to take pictures with us. That's how the word of our ministry in Houston spread. We give God the glory for that manifestation. To top it all off, when we arrived home the tumor under baby Isaiah's tongue had completely disappeared, just as I had spoken it. We didn't have to put this newborn baby through surgery. We thank God often for that miracle.

IN THE GLORY

This next section highlights a few more encounters I experienced in the glory. I cannot list them all because it would take up the whole book.

There was a three-day revival meeting in New Orleans, Louisiana. This was my hometown. I knew that a prophet would not be honored in his own home or city, but I decided to go anyway. When we arrived in New Orleans, from the first day of the meeting the opposition was evident. The event organizer backed out at the last minute, so we didn't have a venue for the meeting. Thankfully, a pastor friend of my sister allowed us to use his church. On the first night of the meeting, very few people showed up, no manifestations took place, and I was discouraged. My wife encouraged me that night after the service and said, "Baby, God didn't bring us out here for nothing. He will show up."

The next night more people showed up, including many of my family members. When I saw my family I was even more desperate for God to show Himself. I knew this was an opportunity for the enemy to make me look false in front of them. The service started, and as I held an altar call my grandma's pants started to fall. She experienced instantaneous weight loss. Then, a lady jumped up to her feet, shouting that she'd just seen money appear in her purse. I had seen miracles like this in Houston before. However, I thought God would have to come down from His throne in order for miracles to happen in a city like New Orleans. These signs and wonders were great, but I knew it would take more than falling pants and money appearing to convince my family.

Without warning, a woman whose husband had run her over with a car just moments earlier crawled into the sanctuary. She was bleeding from various lacerations on her flesh; her arm was broken as well. To top it off, she had a heavy drug smell on her from using crack cocaine. When the pastor saw her, he called for me and said, "Prophet, please help this lady." I went over to pray for her, and I told the people to help stand her up.

What you are about to hear next is a miracle. I've never seen anything like it since. All of a sudden, the lady started to stare into my eyes like she saw something or someone. Her arms popped and straightened out. The skin around her wounds grew back to its original color as we looked at her. She then spoke in fluent tongues and the crack cocaine smell disappeared. She was fully restored.

My family freaked out and backed away from me. From that day forward, some of my family members have feared talking to me. However, it wasn't me—it was the power of God that healed that lady and set her free from her bondage. Thank you, Lord Jesus. Now that's what I call a miracle.

I will tell you about one more encounter I had while transitioning from misery to ministry. I would like to tell you more, but I would need to write five more books just to cover it all.

A friend's church was having a grand opening. So, my wife and I decided to pay a visit. The pastor's wife held an altar call and asked the people who desired a touch from God to come up front. She asked my wife and me to come and pray for the people. We started to pray, and in came a woman with a walker who had been paralyzed by a stroke. I prayed for her, and right before our eyes the woman straightened out her arms and legs and ran around the church. My wife, Tora, prayed for the piano player and he fell under the power of God. Revival broke out; the teenagers in the room started to cry for no reason. The power of God is always recognizable when the youth are touched. Today's youth will not fake it or do courtesy drops. They will not show their emotions unless it is real. In that service, the youth were just as touched as the adults.

There was a woman with a contracted arm—no blood circulated to the affected area of her body. Her doctors were scheduled to perform an amputation surgery the following week. After she saw the paralyzed woman receive her miracle, she was emboldened in her faith and wanted to receive her own miracle. By the grace and anointing of God, her arm loosened and straightened out. She regained full use of her arm and was totally healed.

We have seen God move in many miraculous ways. We have seen a woman healed from twelve tumors on her pancreas; she had been given only three months to live, but God had the final say. We've seen many babies born from barren wombs. A man, blind since birth, received his healing after the anointing of God hit him at one of our services. Ear drums of the deaf have regenerated at our meetings. The crippled have walked and people have been healed from various diseases. One lady was having a seizure in the meeting and God healed her; she had a tumor the size of a boiled egg on her leg and it disappeared.

We have had people receive the following amounts of money in our meetings as I released money miracles into the atmosphere: $287,000.00; $100,000.00; $84,000.00; $50,000.00 on many occasions. One lady came to our meeting just to discredit who I was in the Lord. She said she was there to prove that I was a false prophet. I began to release money miracles in the service and told everyone to check their purses and wallets. So, she checked her purse and nothing was in there. Then, before the service was over I told everyone to check their purses and wallets again. The lady began to check and found several hundred-dollar bills in the shape of an airplane in her purse. She told her testimony and has been following the ministry ever since. If God uses us, He can use anyone. He will turn all your misery into a ministry.

Lord, we thank you for turning our misery into a ministry. I command that everything the enemy has stolen from us since our birth be released now in Jesus' name. Money, thou art loosed and send prosperity now! Thank you for our salvation and deliverance and may shalom peace be released in Jesus' name!

Chapter 3

How to TAP

TAP Through Drinking

When I say TAP through drinking, I am not referring to alcoholic beverages or intoxicating liquor. In this segment, I am addressing the new wine of the Spirit of God.

In the physical realm, wine is an alcoholic drink created from fermented grapes. In the spiritual realm, wine is the outpouring of God's anointing. One passage of Scripture describes wine as such: *"Nor do they put new wine into old wineskins, or else the wineskins break, the wine is spilled, and the wineskins are ruined. But they put new wine into new wineskins, and both are preserved"* (Matt. 9:17 NKJV). One of the problems in the church is that they want new anointing poured into old vessels. This particular Scripture is an explanation about fasting (see Matt. 9:14-16). However, it also outlines a strategy for looking at things differently. To get new wine, we have to get rid of our old ways, old traditions, and old methods. A 1930s message will not be effective in the new millennium. The modern-day church isn't reaching the youth of America today. The reason is that we are preaching an eight-track message to an iPad generation. We must learn to become all things to all men in order to win some souls for the Lord (see 1 Cor. 9:22).

Oftentimes, when wine is involved there is a party or celebration going on. We are so caught up with routine and religion that we neglect our relationship with God and His people. As we read in Luke 2:52, *"Jesus increased in wisdom and stature, and in favour with God and man."* An increase in the anointing brings favor with God and man. Many of us know how to be good sons and daughters to God. However, we are terrible brothers and sisters to one another. We can have favor with God and be heaven bound. However, without favor with man, we will be no earthly good. Jesus Himself, who was God in the flesh, needed favor with man as well. We can be highly anointed, but without the anointing of influence with man no one will support our cause. Jesus told us that people will know we are His by the love we show to each other (see John 13:35). We must learn how to get "drunk" together in the Spirit with kindness, compassion, forgiveness, and unity (see Eph. 4:32).

Many churches host revival meetings or conferences when they are spiritually dry. They say, "Come as you are!" Unfortunately, a majority of attendees leave the same way they came in. The only thing that is revived and renewed is the same watered down, luke-warm spirit. We need something beyond a revival. We need a restructuring. Today's revivalists are looking for God's Spirit to move the way He did in past revivals. However, the Lord wants to do a new thing and pour out new wine.

Those with the Pharisee spirit love to hold on to the traditional way of doing things. They can't wrap their minds around God's new concepts. Anything that seems foreign to their protocol is written off as witchcraft, emotionalism, or just "not of God." The Bible says we are a peculiar people (see 1 Pet. 2:9). I would rather look peculiar to man than be peculiar because of man.

THE WINEPRESS AND HOW WINE IS CREATED

The winepress consisted of an area called the "treading floor." It was often cut from stone and included a drainage hole near the bottom, so that grape juices could flow into the collecting pool beneath the floor. Grapes were then placed on the treading floor where men used their feet to crush them. In Scripture, this process is often associated with the execution of God's wrath. Revelation 19:15 says: *"And out of his mouth goeth a sharp word, that with it he should smite the nations: and he shall rule them with a rod of iron: and he treadeth the winepress of the fierceness and wrath of Almighty God."* Everyone wants the new wine of God's Spirit. However, they don't want the judgment and the spirit of repentance that comes along with it.

In the winemaking process, we have to pick out the grapes, then we have to stomp on them to press out the juice. The Holy Spirit is telling the church the same thing. First, we must get picked out, then we must be picked on, stomped on, and trampled over. God is going to have to squeeze us until all the dross, dryness, and deadness of spirit is taken out of us. Another reason we can't receive new wine is that we haven't made proper use of the old wine yet. Some of us have received impartations that we haven't accessed or used. Most impartations come in seed form, so we must become a glory chaser in order to increase in that particular anointing.

Some impartations do come fully formed. Once an impartation is received, it's the job of the recipient to exercise the gift. Many people think exercising the gift means going out and ministering, laying hands on and prophesying over the people. That's not the case. Exercising the gift involves building up and developing the anointing through fasting, praying, speaking in tongues, and worship. These principles send growth hormones to our spiritual baby (gift) to assist in full-term birthing.

We may be asking ourselves, how do we get the new wine? Below is a scriptural pattern to help us figure this out. John 2:3 reads, *"And when they wanted wine, the mother of Jesus said unto him, 'They have no wine.'"* First, we have to desire and be thirsty in order to get the new wine to come. Second, we must recognize that we have run out of wine. Many pastors, prophets, and evangelists are still active in ministry work. However, they were fired a long time ago.

This is the only job that allows us to work after we've been laid off. People are not getting healed, saved, or set free because the minister is riding on a low tank of gas. We can't take the people far in the spirit when we are running on "E." We must fill up our tank before we offer anyone a ride in the spirit.

Now, it's important to move on to the next step in getting new wine. John 2:5 reads, *"His mother saith unto the servants, Whatsoever he saith unto you, do it."* I want to point out two key points here. First, Jesus' mother spoke to the servants—in order to get the new wine, we need to have a servant's heart and mentality. That mentality was *"Whatsoever he saith unto you, do it."* Some of us might say, "I serve in my church and ministry." That may be true, but do you serve without question and without your own motives or agendas? These servants followed the commands of Jesus' mother without looking for recognition from Jesus. Mary, the mother of Jesus, was not even the servants' master at this wedding. However, because they had servants' hearts, they listened and responded to authority even when they did not have to.

Second, Mary told the servants to do whatever Jesus told them to do. In today's society, individuals will adhere to their pastor's commands more than they adhere to God's commands. This also proves that Mary could not save the wedding or perform any miracles herself. She simply directed the servants to the one and only main source—Jesus. So, for those religions who encourage prayer toward Mary or any other saints to talk to God for them, just remember— Mary referred the people back to Jesus, not herself.

Jesus said, *"No man cometh unto the Father, but by me"* (John 14:6). Going further along in John 2, it tells us in verse 6 that *"There were set there six waterpots of stone, after the manner of the purifying of the Jews, containing two or three firkins apiece."* Remember, the water was there for purification. We must purify ourselves; before God can turn our water into new wine. We must be consecrated, sanctified, and living holy before the Lord. In Second Timothy 2:21, we read, *"If a man therefore purge himself from these, he shall be a vessel unto honour, sanctified, and meet* [useful] *for the master's use, and prepared unto every good work."*

The Lord wants us to demonstrate His power mightily upon the earth. However, we must first be purged. The word *purge* means "to extract" or "to cleanse thoroughly." We must find every known and unknown sin and extract it by force. The Body of Christ must force itself out of sin and into a lifestyle of holiness. Compromising in the realm of sin isn't an option anymore.

Last but not least, John 2:7 says, *"Jesus saith unto them, Fill the waterpots with water. And they filled them up to the brim."* Water signifies the Spirit. Jesus wanted the servants to fill these vessels up with water (the Spirit). We must learn to keep our vessels filled with the

Holy Ghost. Praying in tongues is one way to do this. Jude 1:20 says, *"But ye, beloved, building up yourselves on your most holy faith, praying in the Holy Ghost."* So let's get drunk in the Holy Ghost!

If you have not been baptized in the Holy Spirit, please repeat this prayer:

> *Jesus, I accept you as my Lord and Savior. I believe you died on a cross and rose from the dead. Come into my heart and make me clean from all my sins. I renounce satan and every evil covenant I made with him by indulging in sin. Forgive me. I repent from my evil and disobedient ways. Now, Holy Spirit, I welcome you into my life. Baptize me with your Spirit and fire, and give me the evidence of speaking in tongues because your word said, "If ye then, being evil, know how to give good gifts unto your children: how much more shall your heavenly Father give the Holy Spirit to them that ask Him?" (Luke 11:13). So we declare and decree that it is done in the mighty name of Jesus Christ!*

TAP THROUGH MENTORSHIP

Mentorship is an intriguing part of the Christian walk. A mentor is a counselor who teaches and guides. A mentor deals with the mental—yes, the mentality. *Mentality* means "a habit of the mind." A good mentor will help their subject reshape and redirect the habits of the mind. A mentor will mold and structure the right information or revelation to benefit that individual. Mentors help us to grow and become fruitful.

There is a doctrine that says we don't need to listen to man, only to God. This is true in one sense, but not true in another. Let's look at what the Bible says about this doctrine: *"And he gave some, apostles; and some, prophets; and some, evangelists; and some, pastors and teachers; for the perfecting* [equipping] *of the saints, for the work of the ministry, for the edifying of the Body of Christ"* (Eph. 4:11-12). Many people misinterpret this Scripture. The five-fold ministry equips the saints for the work of ministry; the saints do not equip or perfect themselves. Some might say, "The Holy Spirit teaches me all things" (see 1 John 2:27). It is absolutely true that the Holy Spirit teaches us all things; we must also remember that He often does it through the five-fold ministry. If the Holy Spirit taught us all things only, explain why we don't receive certain revelations or information until a man speaks to us. Whether it was through teaching or prophecy, we receive through a man. If we don't need man's input, then we can just do away with churches, pastors, Bible studies, etc. We can just stay at home and let the Holy Spirit teach us everything.

The Holy Spirit is a gift that has been given to us. However, the five-fold ministry is also a gift. Ephesians 4:7-8 says, *"Unto every one of us is given grace according to the measure of the gift of Christ. Wherefore he saith, When he* [Jesus] *ascended up on high, he led captivity captive, and gave gifts unto men."* We notice Paul speaks in plural form when he says "gifts." A few verses later, he lists those gifts—apostles, prophets, evangelists, pastors, and teachers. So, besides the infilling of the Holy Spirit, Jesus gives the Body of Christ, which is other humans on earth, as tools to assist us in finishing the work of the cross. I would like to stress that when He (Jesus) said *"and gave gifts unto men"* that didn't mean men received gifts. What it actually meant was the men were the gifts given to mankind from God. We are the gift.

Many people eliminate the importance of others from their Christian walk for several reasons. Some may have experienced bad relationships in their childhood or later on in life through an abusive marriage or friendship. Even worse, they may have encountered religious Pharisees in the church who left them with church hurt and distrust in their hearts. This person can be recognized by their insistence that someone is trying to control them. This statement is spoken out of fear of being hurt. Many people mistake order for control and confidence for being cocky. The truth of the matter is, God has given us rules and protocol to follow. This keeps the purpose of His Kingdom decent and in working order. We can find excuses and even Scriptures to justify why we should not trust man. At the end of the day, they don't stand up to a comprehensive study of the subject. Remember, Jesus even had to become a man to save mankind.

There are other biblical examples of mentoring relationships, such as Timothy following Paul. He did not follow Peter, James, John, or the other apostles. Paul was his only mentor. The disciples followed Jesus. Joshua followed Moses. Elisha followed Elijah only; Second Kings 2 tells the story of how Elijah tried to leave Elisha three times—when he went to Bethel, Jericho, then the Jordan. However, the protégé, Elisha, said something powerful to Elijah, the mentor, every time: *"As the Lord liveth, and as thy soul liveth, I will not leave thee"* (2 Kings 2:2,4,6). This singular devotion was the key that led to Elisha receiving the double-portion anointing from Elijah.

Faithfulness is the key to the double-portion anointing. Elisha knew Elijah was going to be taken up; so did the sons of the prophets. Elijah wanted to test Elisha's faithfulness to serve him. Faithfulness is one of the fruits of the spirit found in Galatians 5:22. If the Body of Christ learns how to stick with their leaders to the end, we can receive that leader's mantle. However, we are a microwave generation that wants hands laid on us today, then to go and do healing crusades tomorrow. It doesn't work like that. We must serve and be faithful to the leader and his ministry to receive what he has.

Some of us are saying, "Well, I don't need to wait on man. The Holy Spirit will anoint me." Yes, the Holy Spirit will anoint us; but remember, Elisha asked for a double portion of Elijah's spirit, not the Holy Spirit:

> *And so it was, when they had crossed over, that Elijah said to Elisha, "Ask! What may I do for you, before I am taken away from you?" Elisha said, "Please let a **double portion of your spirit be upon me**." So he said, "You have asked a hard thing. Nevertheless, **if you see me when I am taken from you, it shall be so for you**; but if not, it shall not be so"* (2 Kings 2:9-10 NKJV).

Our individual spirit lives inside of us along with the Holy Spirit. Elisha wanted the attributes and traits of his mentor. He desired Elijah's spirit. That is exactly why Elisha started performing miracles similar to the ones his teacher Elijah did during his earthly ministry. We may all have the Holy Spirit, but we also have different manifestations of the gifts. First Corinthians 12:4 tells us, *"Now there are diversities of gifts, but the same Spirit."* So, yes, we may have some gifts, but not all. Every ministry has its own particular anointing. First Corinthians 14:32 tells us, *"And the spirits of the prophets are subject to the prophets."* If we are called to be a prophet, not only do we need the Holy Spirit but also the spirit of the prophets. According to prophetic Scripture, John the Baptist had the spirit of Elijah (see Mal. 4:5; Luke 1:11-17). We may have the spirit of prophecy and may prophesy. However, that doesn't mean we have the spirit of the prophet that allows us to walk in the office of the prophet. This is what Elisha received from the prophet Elijah—the spirit of the prophet. There is a big difference between the gifts and offices or mantles.

In a previous chapter, I mentioned that we have our majors and our minors in ministry. One ministry's major might be healing, while another's might be prophecy or working of miracles. Ministries that have similar majors will still yield diverse manifestations of those gifts. Some may experience heavy gold dust at their meetings, while others may experience instant weight loss in their meetings. Some may have many sick people healed at their services. Still others will see manifestations of multiple gifts, while others experience a few of them.

Whatever the case may be, if we are under the covering of a ministry we will receive its particular anointing. Remember, the mantle is on the man, not the Holy Spirit. In First Corinthians 12:7 we read, *"But the manifestation of the Spirit is given to every man to profit withal."* Even though the mantle comes from God, it's still assigned to a particular individual or ministry.

The following "Ms" of ministry will help us discern if we are following the right ministry. He must be a man 1) with a *mantle*, 2) with a *message*, 3) with a *mandate*, 4) with a *manifestation*, 5) with a *ministry*, that's 6) on a *mission*, who knows 7) how to *manage his money*. If we don't see all of these qualifications in the one leading the ministry, then we're following the wrong leader.

Before I close this subject, I want to address one last vital point. To avoid being hurt, misused, or lied to, avoid this one mistake. Don't look for a church home or a mentor. Let them find you. Remember, Jesus picked His disciples. In John 15:16 Jesus said, *"Ye have not chosen me, but I have chosen you, and ordained you."* Paul picked Timothy (see Acts 16:1-3). Elijah picked Elisha: *"So he [Elijah] departed thence, and found Elisha the son of Shaphat, who was plowing with twelve yoke of oxen before him, and he with the twelfth: and Elijah passed by him, and cast his mantle upon him"* (1 Kings 19:19).

Our mentor or pastor must find us plowing. He must see if we are worthy of the anointing. Notice that Elijah cast the mantle on Elisha before he actually received it. I believe it was because he wanted to see if it would fit Elisha. Some of us are trying to put on shoes and mantles that don't fit. I tell all my protégés, "You can ask questions, but don't question." It's quite simple—if we know what we are doing, then we don't need a mentor. That's like telling a mechanic who has been fixing cars for years how to fix our vehicle. We must practice the law of the student and learn to listen to authority. If we can grasp this principle and the importance of mentorship, then we can receive a double-portion anointing. So, let's open up our hearts to this principle and TAP.

HANDS-ON TRAINING

The following principle has been misunderstood and misused. It has diminished over the years because of a misinterpretation concerning the glory or glory realm of God. The principle I speak of is the "laying on of hands." "Hand" in Scripture is commonly used and is usually translated from the Hebrew word *yad*, which means power.

Hands have a literal usage but also are spoken of in a figurative sense. In Genesis 9:2, the word *hand* infers strength or power: *"And the fear of you and the dread of you shall be upon every beast of the earth, and upon every fowl of the air, upon all that moveth upon the earth, and upon all the fishes of the sea; into your hand are they delivered."* Deliverance lies in the power of the hand, whether it is God's hand or human hands. Genesis 48:14 illustrates another use of hands: *"And Israel stretched out his right hand, and laid it upon Ephraim's head, who was the younger, and his left hand upon Manasseh's head, guiding his hands wittingly; for Manasseh was the firstborn."* This laying on of the hands signifies blessings and ordination. Without the laying on of hands in the Old and New Testaments, one was not officially anointed or appointed by the elders for that position, office, or gifting. We find a clear example of this in First Timothy 4:14: *"Neglect not the gift that is in thee, which was given thee by prophecy, with the laying on of the hands of the presbytery."* A gift of the Spirit was given by physical contact through the laying on of hands. It wasn't given just by asking for it, but through the point of contact from the elders' hands to release the impartation.

In this verse, the gift was also given through prophecy. We can prophecy over someone. However, without the laying on of hands, the ceremony, ordination, or the gifting is not complete. We also see this in Acts 13:2-3: *"As they ministered to the Lord, and fasted, the Holy Ghost said, Separate me Barnabas and Saul for the work whereunto I have called them. And when they had fasted and prayed, and laid their hands on them, they sent them away."*

Saul and Barnabas didn't become great apostles of the faith until prayer, fasting, and the laying on of hands was administered to them. The Holy Spirit spoke the calling, but man commissioned them through the laying on of hands. I see many women and men of God who have walked away from this practice. There are ministers who are convinced that worship and the atmosphere of glory will cause miracles to take place. This is true to a certain degree. However, I have also observed many who came to a meeting for healing and left the meeting still diseased, blind, in wheelchairs, and not delivered. These ministers make excuses saying it's up to the Lord to heal them or that the atmosphere of worship wasn't right.

As mentioned earlier, when Jesus walked the earth He did not have a worship service before He administered healing. He often laid hands on people. Matthew 17:16-17 tells us of a father crying out to Jesus to deliver his son: *"And I brought him to thy disciples, and they could not cure him. Then Jesus answered and said, O faithless and perverse generation, how long shall I be with you? how long shall I suffer you? bring him hither to me."* If Jesus rebuked the disciples for not being able to cast out devils during His earthly ministry, I wonder what He thinks of the modern-day church. When someone doesn't get healed, we often shift the blame to God. However, it's God's will for everyone to be healed, set free, and delivered. We as Christians must start owning up to the part we play in the deliverance, healing, and wholeness of the people. If we took more time to minister to people through the laying on of hands, we would see more healings take place. Jesus gave us a good example in Luke 4:40: *"Now when the sun was setting, all they that had any sick with diverse diseases brought them unto him; and he laid his hands on every one of them, and healed them."*

We often use the excuse that we can't lay hands on everybody, especially when we have large crowds. However, Jesus did it. Some estimate that the crowd spoken of in Luke 4:40 consisted of several thousand people. I understand that circumstances sometimes prevent us from laying hands on everyone. However, if we have the opportunity, we should lay hands on those who are really in need of prayer.

So why should we lay hands on people? *"Lay hands suddenly on no man, neither be partaker of other men's sins: keep thyself pure"* (1 Tim. 5:22). Many think this Scripture means that we should not be quick to lay hands on anyone, which is true. However, in context it means not to be so quick to commission anyone, especially those who are in sin. This does not refer to those who need healing administered to them. Jesus did not lay hands on everyone either, some only received their healing through their relentless faith (see Matt. 15:22-28). But for the most part, He laid hands on thousands of people.

It was through the laying on of hands of the apostles that the Holy Spirit was given and the people received the gift of tongues. Simon the sorcerer realized this and wrongly desired to buy God's freely given gift. Jesus told His disciples to remember, *"Freely ye have received, freely give*" (Matt. 10:8). Simon the sorcerer wanted to buy the gift from the apostles, saying, "*Give me also this power, that on whomsoever I lay hands, he may receive the Holy Ghost*" (Acts 8:19).

Simon the sorcerer even caught the revelation that the power was administered through the laying on of the apostles' hands. If a sorcerer can grasp this principle, why can't we? Think about it. In a lot of churches, many people get born again, but never receive the Holy Spirit. If they do, it's often later on from another ministry or an invited evangelist. Perhaps it's because we have altar calls without laying on hands for the baptism of the Holy Spirit. These days, people have adapted to allowing the sovereign atmosphere to do everything for them. Jesus said the power is in the hand, so why don't we use this point of contact for healing, miracles, signs, and wonders?

As I indicated before, the Hebrew word *yad*, which is most often translated as "hand," means strength or power. To understand this theory, we must first understand what God's hand does: "*Thy right hand, O Lord, is become glorious in power: thy right hand, O Lord, hath dashed in pieces the enemy*" (Exod. 15:6). We see here that God's right hand is where His power lies. Luke 22:69 confirms this: "*Hereafter shall the Son of man sit on the right hand of the power of God.*" The right hand of God is His power source, and the Son of man sits on that side. Who is that Son of man? It is none other than Jesus, of course. Again, I am not saying the Lord doesn't heal without hands being laid. We have seen multitudes of miracles, healings, and deliverances without touching a single person. However, we have also seen many not healed because the minister refused to lay hands. If someone doesn't get healed, they say it wasn't God's timing or blame it on the atmosphere not being strong enough. Then some say the people lack faith. When we look at Mark 6:5-6, it states that even Jesus had to apply this principle when the faith level wasn't conducive. It reads:

"He [Jesus] *could not do any miracles there, except lay his hands on a few sick people and heal them. He was amazed at their lack of faith"* (NIV).

Jesus knew their faith wasn't at the level to receive sovereign miracles. However, He didn't refuse the people their healing because He refused to lay hands. He kicked into gear two and started administering the glory through the point of contact with His hands. Many believe that when ministers lay hands, they are operating in the anointing, not the glory of God. This is far from the truth. The laying on of hands is just another way to minister in the glory. The reason many people get tired when they administer the glory through laying on of hands is because they are ministering through the flesh, not the spirit. For this reason, the laying on of hands has received a bad reputation.

I have ministered under the glory with laying on of hands to hundreds and even thousands of people in one night without getting tired. To put this in perspective, we realize that we must ask the Lord to stretch His hands out to enforce His power on our enemies (see Acts 4:29-30). We also know that allowing the Lord sovereign healing is always best. However, I want us to look inside ourselves and see if we are doing our part as well. A time might come when we cannot wait to do miracles until a band or worship leader sings the right songs.

The Holy Spirit does not minister the glory or anointing the same way all the time. One day, He might tell us to lay hands; the next day He might say, "Just proclaim the written Word." No one has a patent on the Holy Spirit. Even Jesus did not minister the same way all the time. Remember, *"But all these worketh that one and selfsame Spirit, dividing to every man severally as he will"* (1 Cor. 12:11). It's at His will, not our will, so we don't determine how He will perform it. We must get out of our routine and get back to the simplicity of the Gospel. No matter how much new revelation we get about the glory realm or other realms. We can never take away Jesus' methods and commandments for how we should administer miracles as believers. He is the best example of how to perform miracles. Read Mark 16:15-18 and TAP.

Again, this section of the book wasn't intended to insult or undermine anyone who doesn't administer the laying on of hands. It is meant to encourage us to go back to the days of our first love, before we learned about the atmospheric realms. The days when we oiled up everything we saw and were willing to even lay hands on our pets. This section was also not meant to give any man praise. It is meant to help us recognize the role we play in the gifts of the Spirit being released. The Lord cannot break the jurisdiction He gave us. Jurisdiction means the lawful right or power to interpret and apply the law of the territory within which that power is exercised. God gave us dominion in this jurisdiction (see Gen. 1:26-28). He had to become man to save man. The job is up to us; we have the power and that power is in our hands.

TAP THROUGH TV

I love watching Christian television. I was a new believer with a supernatural assignment, so I needed a mentor who moved in the supernatural. It was rare to find people in my city who moved in the glory. A lot of churches had good entertainment, but they didn't have the revelation about the atmospheric anointing. I use to show up in churches talking about manifestations of gold dust, and they thought I had gone off the deep end. So, I was forced to watch Christian television and the Internet to learn more about the supernatural.

The show *It's Supernatural!* with Sid Roth caught my attention above the rest of the programs. I watched the show and saw average people moving in the anointing and making it sound and look so easy. I became a believing and faithful fan, watching the show every time it aired. Then, I would go on the Internet and watch the archives. One day, I watched Pastor Tony Kemp on the show. He said he had watched archived shows just like me. He then had the chance to meet someone from the show who gave him in-depth mentoring about the supernatural. Before he knew it, he was on the show talking about his own encounters in the supernatural. I said to myself, "I am going to do the same thing that guy did."

Months passed and my friend told me that he had a dream that Sid Roth came to him and said, "Shawn has a book he needs to write about the supernatural." When he told me about the dream I was excited. However, I brushed it off because I didn't know the first thing about writing a book. I could barely read, so I knew it was just another pipe dream. Two years passed and my ministry started to progress. I started running into people at conferences who were former guests on *It's Supernatural!* with Sid Roth.

One day, I was at a meeting in Dallas with David Herzog, and the Holy Spirit gave me an acronym. He said, *"TAP—The Anointed Principles."* Electricity went through my body. He said, *"This is the book I want you to write. Start now!"* My friend Joel was with me during that encounter, and the Lord reminded us of the dream he had two years prior.

Then, I met Kathie Walters. She walked up to me, touched me with her right index finger, and said, "Oh, a prophet!" I was almost knocked back. The people behind me felt the power surge. She told me, "If I touch you with my left hand, it means you're just walking in the gift. However, if I touch you with my right hand, you're walking in that office of that gift." Then, she rebuked me for having a religious spirit. I took it with love. She is such a funny lady.

Mahesh Chavda prophesied over my wife and me concerning our ministry and my book. He also talked about how powerful our ministry would be and said he wanted the first copy of my book when it was finished. Leif Hetland prophesied that I would go to the nations. John Kilpatrick prophesied over me and said, *"When you preach, you will have fire in your heart and tears in your eyes."* Glenda Jackson and I are working together to open up the wells of revival. Joan Hunter and I became good friends. She is an awesome woman of God and I was ordained under her healing ministry. Tony Kemp and I finally met. It was like history repeating itself. He agreed to be a spiritual mentor to me, and he taught me a lot. Last but not least, Pastor James and Gloria Durham have become like spiritual parents to me. They have a lot a wisdom and love of God. I love them and I thank them for helping me to TAP!

> *Lord I pray for those who have read some of these principles that I used to TAP into your spiritual blessings. May they receive them with ease and guide them into all truth on their spiritual journey to obtain the fullness of God.*

TAP!

Chapter 4

COMMUNION PRINCIPLES

THE POWER OF COMMUNION

In this chapter, I will explain the importance of communion, or communication with the Holy Spirit. I will also elaborate on the Holy Spirit's vital role in the day-to-day activities in a believer's walk with the Lord. During this process of evaluation of the Spirit, we will receive an impartation for more of the Holy Spirit's presence in our lives. In this section, we will TAP into the world of the Holy Spirit.

The word "communion" is translated from the Greek word *koinonia*, and it is defined as "partnership or association, spiritual fellowship or intimacy," or "benefaction." A benefaction is a charitable donation or gift. Communion with the Holy Spirit is not just sharing words; it is also a gift. Therefore, we must reciprocate the gift of communion or communication to show our appreciation for Him. Communion also means a "mutual sharing of feelings and thoughts." In the Greek language, *koinonia* also means "partnership." The word *partnership* means "two or more persons who run a business together and share in the profits and losses." Wow! So that means, we are business partners and co-CEOs with the Holy Spirit. We help oversee the daily operations of Father God's business with Him. Mark 16:20 reads, *"And they went forth, and preached every where, the Lord working with them, and confirming the word with signs following."* This Scripture tells us the Lord was working *with* them, not *for* them. We work with the Lord as business partners, not as employees. Once we understand our proper position in the Kingdom, we will see the benefits of that position.

The Body of Christ has a slothful spirit. They expect the Lord to do Kingdom business *for* them. There is an excuse they love to use to explain this dilemma: "I am just waiting on the Lord." I hate to be a burden breaker, but the Lord is waiting on us to get to work. The Body of Christ doesn't understand this concept because the traditions of men have taught us that we can't get God to move when we want Him to. Growing up, I was taught that we can't talk to God the wrong way because He might strike us down. But, once I was filled with the Holy Spirit and began to dig into the Word for myself, I realized that God allows people to express their feelings to Him and negotiate with Him.

Here are some scriptural examples.

Abraham

> *And the Lord said, Shall I hide from Abraham that thing which I do* (Genesis 18:17).

In this passage, the Lord was on the verge of destroying Sodom and Gomorrah for their sins. However, before He made a decision on the earth He consulted with His business partner first—yes, Abraham—who in response started to negotiate with God. The following verse tells us about the end of these negotiations.

> *And he said, Oh let not the Lord be angry, and I will speak yet but this once: Peradventure ten shall be found there. And he said, I will not destroy it for ten's sake. And the Lord went His way, as soon as he had left* **communing with Abraham**: *and Abraham returned unto his place* (Genesis 18:32-33).

This emphasizes the power of communication or communion. Abraham negotiated with God on Sodom and Gomorrah's behalf. On the strength of Abraham the Lord would have spared those cities, if He had found righteousness.

The Gentile Woman

> *But he answered and said, It is not meet to take the children's bread, and to cast it to dogs. And she said, Truth, Lord: yet the dogs eat of the crumbs which fall from their master's table. Then Jesus answered and said unto her, O woman, great is thy faith: be it unto thee even as thou wilt. And her daughter was made whole from that very hour* (Matthew 15:26-28).

This Gentile woman was not even in covenant with God. However, her faith opened the door of communication, and she began to negotiate with God. Even though it wasn't in His will to reach out to her, the relentless faith gave her an audience with Jesus. In Matthew 15:24, He stated, *"I am not sent but unto the lost sheep of the house of Israel."* This Gentile woman knew how to communicate with God through the faith principle; she was able to change the heart, mind, and assignment of God.

Hezekiah

Hezekiah prayed thirty words and the Lord changed His mind and gave him fifteen more years of life. We can find that story in Second Kings 20:1-6. If we get the understanding that the Lord wants us to communicate with Him honestly and even emotionally in the spirit, then and only then we will see more manifestations of the Spirit in the earth realm. So let's TAP!

WHO IS THE HOLY SPIRIT?

Before we embark on the journey of discovering the origins and attributes of the Holy Spirit, I am going to define what He is not. I like this description of the Holy Spirit:

> He is not water (tho' refreshes like one), wind (tho' He moves like one), fire (tho' He purifies like one) or white dove (tho' He is gentle like one); He is not an "it" but rather a Him. He is a person not a presence.[1]

He is an actual person with a presence.

Many view the Holy Spirit as an energy force from God that gets released into the atmosphere when we are in a church service. Some identify Him as the goosebumps or emotional reactions that people receive during a time of worship. I grew up with a traditional Baptist background. When someone would "catch the Holy Ghost" in a service, the ushers would begin to fan him or her. They would escort that person out of the building if he or she became too much of a distraction. People, me included, would turn around in our seats staring at this person like he or she had just lost it. But, even as a little boy I questioned, "If that is the Holy Ghost, why would they escort God out of the building?" I asked myself, "If that's not the

Holy Ghost and it's just emotionalism," I wanted to know, "who was the Holy Ghost and how does He operate?"

NEEDING TO KNOW HIM

In the previous segment, I explained who the Holy Spirit is not. So, let me share what I have learned about who He is from my own knowledge, experiences, and encounters with Him. The Holy Spirit is the third person of the triune Godhead. Matthew 28:19 and Second Corinthians 13:14 speak of the three—Father, Son, and the Holy Spirit. The word *spirit* in the Old Testament is almost always the translation of the Hebrew word *ruach*, as in Zechariah 4:6: "*This is the word of the Lord unto Zerubbabel, saying, Not by might, nor by power, but by my spirit, saith the Lord of hosts.*" The word *ruach* means "breath, wind, touch" or "to make a quick understanding of." In the New Testament, "spirit" is translated from the Greek word *pneuma*, similar in meaning to *ruach* in the Hebrew.

I understand now why ministers blow their breath on the audience and say words like "touch," and the crowd feels a tangible reaction of the Spirit manifesting in an unearthly matter. It is possible that the Holy Spirit is using the minister as a host to make those gestures and statements, such as "touch," so He can introduce Himself to the people. We must understand that the Holy Spirit is not just the average spirit we may see in a horror movie or a paranormal activity show. What makes the Holy Spirit stand out in a class of His own? The answer is, He is holy!

What is holy? "Holy" is translated from a Hebrew word *qadosh*, which means "observe as clean, "to consecrate, purify, or sanctify oneself wholly." Similarly, in the New Testament, the Greek word *hagios* means "sacred and set apart for God." All definitions paint a beautiful picture of what the Holy Spirit means to us in our walk with God. The infilling and communion with the Holy Spirit is a vital part of our lives once we receive Jesus Christ as our Savior. In fact, it is only through the drawing of the Father's Spirit, the Holy Spirit, that we can come to Jesus. In John 6:44, Jesus said, *"No man can come to me, except the Father which hath sent me draw him; and I will raise him up at the last day."* How will He draw and raise us up? Of course, He can only draw us through the Holy Spirit. Romans 8:11 says: *"But if the Spirit of him that raised up Jesus from the dead dwell in you, he that raised up Christ from the dead shall also quicken your mortal bodies by his Spirit that dwelleth in you."*

It's the Holy Spirit who raises us from the dead. These are some of the many Scripture references that show the importance of the Holy Spirit before and after the born-again conversion. Most ministers of the Gospel preach on Jesus, and that's what they should preach. However, once that takes place we must emphasize the importance of the Holy Spirit. This must be done so we can access the power of Jesus that will enable that new believer to stay the course. The Holy Spirit is like the invisible pretend friend we had when we were little children. The only difference is, He is real and He answers back when we commune with Him. The Holy Spirit wants to feed us the nutrients of God's presence. However, we must fellowship and partake of this meal through communication. Remember, a closed mouth does not get fed.

GOD, THE HOLY SPIRIT, AND JESUS

We are three-part beings just like God is according to First Thessalonians 5:23: *"I pray God your whole spirit and soul and body be preserved blameless."* We were made in God's image according to Genesis 1:26-27. The beginning of verse 26 says: *"And God said, Let us make man in our image, after our likeness."* Notice that God said *"our"* and *"us."* He referred to Himself in a plural sense. Those who were in attendance at this meeting were God the Father, God the Son, and God the Holy Spirit. He was conversing with all three, even though He was speaking to Himself.

Matthew 28:19 reads, *"Go ye therefore, and teach all nations, baptizing them in the name of the Father, and of the Son, and of the Holy Ghost."* He said to baptize them in the *"name,"* not *"names."* This word is singular, not plural. The Lord is making the statement that He has only one name but three personalities. Well, what name should we use then—God, Jesus, or the Holy Spirit?

> *Wherefore* **God hath** *highly exalted him [Jesus], and* **given him a name** *which is* **above every name***. That at the* **name of Jesus** *every knee should bow, of things in* **heaven***, and things in* **earth***, and things under the earth; and that every tongue should confess that* **Jesus Christ is Lord,** *to the glory of God the Father* (Philippians 2:9-11).

Acts 2:38 tells us, *"Then Peter said unto them, Repent, and be baptized every one of you in the name of Jesus Christ for the remission of sins, and ye shall receive the gift of the Holy Ghost."* Pay attention to what the apostle Peter did—he received the commission from Jesus to baptize in the name of the Father, Son, and Holy Spirit. So, why did he baptize these people in Acts 2:38 only in the name of Jesus and not God or the Holy Spirit? Was Peter backsliding and rebelling against God? The answer is no. See, Peter caught the revelation that Jesus Christ was all three of the Godhead in one according to Colossians 2:9, *"In Him dwelleth all the fullness of the Godhead bodily."* Jesus was God the Father, God the Son, and God the Spirit in one body.

In Romans 13:14, He is referred to as the *"Lord Jesus Christ."* Lord is a translation of the Greek *kurios*, meaning "master, sir, or owner." *Jesus* in the Greek is *Iesous*, which is translated from the Hebrew word *Yehoshua/Jehoshua*—contracted to *Joshua* means "Jehovah/Yahweh saves." *Christ* is from the Greek word *Christos*, which means "the anointed one" or "the Messiah," a description of God's Spirit. Above, I referenced Acts 2:38 which reads: *"And ye shall receive the gift of the Holy Ghost."* Therefore, if we get baptized in the name of Jesus Christ for remission of sins, we will receive the gift of the Holy Spirit. Why would we need the Holy Spirit if we already have the fullness of the Godhead when we receive Jesus? The answer is, we receive God in our heart when we receive Jesus. However, when we receive the infilling of the Holy Spirit by accepting God's gift, we receive power to operate the way Jesus did on the earth. It's the icing on the cake.

JESUS NEEDED HIM

In today's society, New Testament, modern-day believers know that we cannot cast out demons or do great exploits for God unless it's through the name of Jesus Christ. However, I would like to propose a question: what name did Jesus use to cast out demons and heal the sick during His earthly ministry? There is no indication in any of the gospels that He used a name when performing miracles. There is also no indication of a name that Old Testament prophets may have used. Prophets of old had no knowledge of the name of Jesus during their time. Jesus did not use His own name when casting out spirits either. We must wonder—where did their source of power for performing miracles come from without the usage of a name?

Look at Matthew 12:28, where Jesus makes this statement, *"But if I cast out devils by the Spirit of God, then the kingdom of God is come unto you."* Jesus performed miracles through the power of the Holy Spirit. He revealed the Spirit of God as His source of power.

Unfortunately, in modern-day society we tend to ignore the sufficiency of the Holy Spirit. Jesus was saying, "I have my power and my ministry because of the Spirit of God." Jesus was saying that when the Spirit of God moves, the whole Kingdom of God moves. Did we get that? When the Spirit of God moves, the whole Kingdom of God moves.

Mark 1:10-12 tells us:

> *And straightway coming up out of the water, he saw the heavens opened, and **the Spirit** like a dove descending upon him: and there came a **voice from heaven**, saying, Thou art my beloved Son, in whom I am well pleased. And immediately **the spirit driveth him** [Jesus] into the wilderness.*

It wasn't until the Spirit descended like a dove that John heard the voice that claimed Jesus as His Son. It was the voice of the Spirit. We as humans cannot handle the voice of God the Father. It must be filtered through the voice of the Holy Spirit for us to handle it in the natural. His voice is thunderous and His works are so great we can't comprehend them (see Job 37:5). God voice is so powerful that the children of Israel thought they would die if they kept listening to it (see Exod. 20:18). This is why we need to have the Holy Spirit—He is that still small voice in First Kings 19:12. Remember, it's a still small voice, not a loud racing voice that we are used to. See, we must become still and quiet to hear His voice in that capacity. We must learn to break away from the busyness of life, to spend that time tuning into the frequency of heaven. God is always speaking. However, we are too busy to listen. We can be driven by ministry and not driven by His voice. If we faithfully obey the voice of God and do all He commands us to do, these blessings will come upon us and overtake us (see Deut. 28:1-2). The more we tune in the communication station of God's Spirit, the more blessed we become on the earth. So, how can we hear God's voice more clearly besides getting quiet? I'm glad you asked.

PRAY THE FATHER

John 14:16 is a very interesting passage of Scripture that reads: *"And I will pray the Father, and he shall give you another Comforter, that he may abide with you for ever."* I love the first part of this verse. Jesus said, *"I will pray the Father."* This verse is referring to a particular prayer Jesus was going to administer to His disciples. However, why did He state it in that way? One day, I asked the Holy Spirit what Jesus was saying here. The Holy Spirit revealed to me that the statement *"I will pray the Father"* meant He would pray in the Holy Spirit. Praying in the Holy Spirit is praying directly to the Father (see 1 Cor. 14:2).

To explain further, Jesus was aware of the gift of tongues because in Mark 16:17 it reads, *"And these signs shall follow them that believe; In my name shall they cast out devils; they shall speak with new tongues."* Before His ascension, Jesus was explaining to His disciples the detailed manifestation of a true believer. Remember, the disciples had already been operating in certain gifts such as casting out demons and healing the sick (see Matt. 10:1-8). However, the manifestation of speaking in tongues had not been revealed to them yet. In Acts 2:38, Peter told the crowd to repent and be baptized and receive the Holy Spirit. Peter knew that Jesus had told them what a New Testament believer would look like in Mark 16:17. Also, we see it in Acts 19:2, where Paul asked certain disciples in Ephesus if they had received the Holy Ghost after believing. Paul was asking them if they had been baptized in the Holy Spirit. Baptism was the subject at hand (see Acts 19:3). It was customary at that time for a New Testament believer to receive the baptism of the Holy Spirit.

During this encounter, an experience took place. Acts 19:6 tells us, *"And when Paul had laid his hands upon them, the Holy Ghost came on them; and they spake with tongues, and prophesied."*

Speaking in tongues was the prayer language Jesus spoke of in Mark 16:17. However, note that Jesus would not want us to have something He did not know about or do Himself. In First Peter 2:21, it says, *"For even hereunto were ye called: because Christ also suffered for us, leaving us an example, that ye should follow his steps."* This Scripture tells us that He left us an example. In Mark 16, He left an explanation of the sign that would differentiate between those who were His and those who were not. However, is there an earthly example of Jesus using tongues in Scripture? Yes, there is. In John 11:33, the Scripture says, *"When Jesus therefore saw her weeping, and the Jews also weeping which came with her, he groaned in the spirit, and was troubled."* Wow! Jesus groaned in the spirit, not in the flesh. Is there another New Testament Scripture that describes this groaning in the Spirit encounter?

If we examine Romans 8:26, we will see the following Scripture: *"Likewise the Spirit also helpeth our infirmities: for we know not what we should pray for as we ought: but the Spirit itself maketh intercession for us with groanings which cannot be uttered."* This verse indicates to us that groaning is connected to prayer, the Holy Spirit, and intercession. It even ties in to Ephesians 6:18, which states: *"Praying always with all prayer and supplication in the Spirit, and watching there unto with all perseverance and supplication for all saints."*

In the Old Testament, "supplication" is often translated from the Hebrew word *techinnah*, which originates from the word *chanan*, meaning "to petition, to show favor, or to have mercy." Therefore, it would make sense that Jesus was making supplication as He groaned in the Spirit for Lazarus. He favored him and showed him mercy. It hurt Jesus when Lazarus died; the Bible tells us, *"Jesus wept"* (John

11:35). In John 11:33, Jesus groaned in the spirit, and after that He wept in John 11:35. So, we cannot associate groaning and weeping as the same thing. Remember, both were done at separate time frames of the Scripture. After Jesus groaned in the Spirit, in the very next sentence He said, *"Where have ye laid him?"* (John 11:34). Immediately after He groaned in the Spirit, He was ready to go raise the dead.

Jude 1:20 speaks of this kind of action. It reads, *"But ye, beloved, building up yourselves in your most holy faith, praying in the Holy Ghost."* It takes the gift of faith to raise the dead, which is triggered by praying or groaning in the Spirit. This was the same gift of faith the apostle of faith Smith Wigglesworth was known for in his ministry. He raised many people from the dead. Smith was a man who constantly prayed in the Spirit. Jesus gave us a principle to follow so we can perform great miracles. If we can look past our theological mind-sets then maybe, just maybe, we can see how praying in the Holy Ghost was applied by Jesus at the tomb of Lazarus. So, as we *"pray the Father,"* we should start seeing the dead rise in our churches, hospitals, streets, neighborhoods, and outreaches.

Let's learn how to commune with the Holy Spirit and understand His vital importance to our lives. So, according to Second Corinthians 13:14: *"May the grace of the Lord Jesus Christ, and the love of God, and the fellowship of the Holy Spirit be with you all"* (NIV). Thank you, Holy Spirit—you are the guiding force in our lives, and from this day forward we will honor you more, in Jesus name we pray.

> *I pray in the name of Jesus Christ that everyone who reads this chapter and prays gets baptized in the Holy Ghost and fire! Lord, according to Luke 11:13:*

If ye then, being evil, know how to give good gifts unto your children: how much more shall your heavenly Father give the Holy Spirit to them that ask him?

Receive the Holy Spirit, and begin to speak in tongues as the spirit gives utterance.

NOTE

1. Timothy Kyara, "The 3 Most Important Things in Your Life: Mike Murdock," Enroute to Financial Freedom, February 16, 2011, https://timkyara.wordpress.com/books-i-am-reading/the-3-most-important-things-in-your-life-mike-murdock.

Chapter 5

WORSHIP PRINCIPLES

WHAT ARE LEVELS OF WORSHIP?

There are different levels of worship that we can experience in the realm of God's presence. Each level will give us a different outlook and understanding of the principles of worship.

A level is a position from which other heights and depths are measured. There are measurements in the spirit world that determine access into the unseen realms.

To access the spirit of faith, for instance, Jude 1:20 tells us, *"Building up yourselves on your most holy faith, praying in the Holy Ghost."* To *build* means "to fashion or create; to develop or add to." The Body of Christ uses the term *Kingdom building*. We must first build up that place where the King is. So, I ask the question, "Where is the King?" Well, according to Luke 17:21, *"Neither shall they say, Lo here!*

or, lo there! for, behold, the kingdom of God is within you." We must consider the truth that the Kingdom of God is within us. If we are torn to pieces on the inside, God's Kingdom within us is torn up as well. Therefore, we must rebuild the temple of God (see 1 Cor. 6:19). Then we must figure out the depth, width, and height of how to reconstruct His Kingdom. So, how do we do that? The answer is through worship. Let me explain why.

WHERE TO WORSHIP

John 4:20-21 tells us, "*Our fathers worshipped in this mountain; and ye say, that in Jerusalem is the place where men ought to worship. Jesus saith unto her, Women, believe me, the hour cometh, when ye shall neither in this mountain, nor yet at Jerusalem, worship the Father.*" We see in this Scripture that the worship of God is not limited to a structure or geographical location. Oftentimes, pastors and leaders across the world believe their building or church is the dwelling place of the Holy Spirit. However, the truth of the matter is, He dwells in the vessels who worship Him "*in spirit and in truth*" (John 4:23). It's not a building made by the hands of man. It's the individual Kingdom structure within us that determines the level of worship to which God will manifest His presence on earth.

Many people worship out of emotionalism and not in spirit and truth. Anyone can praise God, but only a true worshiper can worship God. I can give a homeless man a dollar, and he will scream *praise the Lord*. However, that does not mean he has the credentials of a worshiper or even have a relationship with God. Psalms 150:6 says, "*Let everything that hath breath praise the Lord. Praise ye the Lord.*" Anyone or anything that can breathe will praise God eventually. However, not everything or everyone will worship Him. It takes a certain kind of individual to worship God. That person must have a personal relationship with God to have access to that type of communication. Not everyone communes with God on that level. However, everyone can if they get in position to. A true worshiper can be recognized by the aroma of heaven that they carry on their lives. Their description of God is a totally different viewpoint than an average believer. We can hear in their conversation the level of intimacy they have for God, especially when a subject about Him comes up. True worshipers are crybabies. A person who has been behind the veil and has entered into the Holy of Holies with God carries a longing in their heart to be with Him again. Nothing else matters to them. They will cry at the drop of a hat just mentioning Him.

In John 4:23, we see the Scripture tells us that "*the Father seeketh such to worship him.*" In worship, we may seek God. However, it is not true worship until God the Father starts to seek us. When we seek the Father, it ignites a spiritual chain reaction that He cannot resist. When we are seeking God in worship, it is almost like we are courting Him. God then finds it hard not to respond to or participate in the courtship. It is similar to experiencing an energy that is identical to the love a mother bestows upon her children. Or like newlyweds on a honeymoon who are deeply in love. Now, it's no longer just us seeking the Father; He is seeking after us.

Think about how important it is to be in a two-sided relationship. A sign that we have reached the vital point in the peak of worship is when our physical being experiences a numbing sensation. During this process, the atmosphere will grow silent and we will tune out the sounds of earthly activities. The weight of God's glory will feel heavy upon our bodies until we can't move. We will begin passing through glorious clouds of light, and electrical currents will go through our physical body. Our awareness of chronological time will diminish as we embark on this journey to a *kairos* moment with

God. This is when we know we have broken through the flesh barrier and entered into that holy place. The more in depth and intense the worship is, the more the Lord reveals His glory to us. When we get into God's personal space through worship, He then gets into our personal affairs through blessings.

DIFFERENT FACETS

In this section of the chapter, we will discuss the different facets of worship. Facets are different aspects or views of a person or subject. Our particular subject is worship. The word *worship* means "reverence for a sacred object" or "high esteem or devotion for a person." According to the biblical and spiritual view, *worship* means to "bow down, prostrate, or do obeisance to." It can also mean "to honor," "reverence," or "to pay homage to superior beings or powers such as men, angels, or God." It's most often used as an honor system paid to a deity, whether it is God or satan (the devil). It can also be either a private or public acknowledgment of that divine presence.

In the Bible, the Israelite patriarchs demonstrated the various stages of worship when they gave reverence to God and sacrificed to Him. They advanced from altars of the Tabernacle and finally they built the Temple. The altars were built of stone and used by both individuals and groups in simple acts of worship and reverence. In both the Tabernacle and the Temple, worship was organized with a complex system of rituals and sacrifices that God outlined for Moses on Mount Sinai. The Temple was built during the reign of King Solomon. The Tabernacle was a portable sanctuary, or tent, that served as a place of worship for the Israelites while they wandered in the wilderness. Both the Tabernacle and the Temple typified God's dwelling with His people.

The Tabernacle, crafted specifically from God's instructions to Moses, stood in a court 150 feet long and 75 feet wide. The sides were covered with linen curtains fastened to sixty pillars of bronze. In the court were the altar of burnt offerings and the bronze laver that was used by the priests for ritual absolutions. The 45- by 15-foot wooden Tabernacle stood at the west end of the court. Inside was a veil that divided it into two parts—the Holy Place and the Holy of Holies. The Lord explained to me one day why He showed up so powerfully in the early 1900s and the '40s and '50s revivals. These meetings were so great because they were held in tents. The Lord said, *"I have always dwelt in tents."* Now He dwells in the tents of man's heart. He showed me how the linens of the Tabernacle resembled king-sized bedsheets, typifying the private and intimate time He spends with His bride through worship.

The Lord told me that without this intimacy with the bridegroom, we cannot produce a breakthrough or a move of God. Also, we cannot birth out powerful ministries without this encounter. He explained to me how many people love the "wedding" of getting born again. However, they don't spend time in worship to get sanctified for the "honeymoon." The wedding is a one-time occasion, but the honeymoon is supposed to be an ongoing event. That is why the familiar passage in Ephesians 5:25-27 reads: *"Husbands, love your wives, even as Christ also loved the church, and gave himself for it; that he might sanctify and cleanse it with the washing of the water by the word, that he might present it to himself a glorious church, not having spot, or wrinkle, or any such thing; but that it should be holy and without blemish."*

I said to myself when I read this Scripture, "The Lord is coming back for a supermodel wife!"

So I asked the Lord, "How can I become that kind of bride for you?"

He responded, "By becoming a worshiper."

Hebrews 10:2 reads: *"For then would they [sacrifices] not have ceased to be offered? because that the worshippers once purged should have had no more conscience of sins."* Wow! There is a purging through worship and a removal of the sin conscience. Through becoming a true worshiper, I can develop the characteristics and image of the bride described in Ephesians 5:25-27. Becoming a worshiper is a lifestyle change. A true worshiper cannot have the same compromises as an average believer, and no believer should have any compromising in their lives anyway. However, a worshiper is held to a high degree of accountability. Worshipers are the ones who have tasted the essence of His presence. So when sin is around, they feel the emptiness or a lift of His presences in their lives. They are the atmosphere carriers of His presence on earth. Without worshipers in our churches, the manifestations of God dry up. Once that happens our gathering places become cemeteries instead of sanctuaries.

DIFFERENT APPROACHES

The word *approach* means "to come near to or draw closer." In the next few sentences, I will define and give us revelation on different approaches to worship. Matthew 4:9-10 reads: *"And saith unto him, All these things will I give thee, if thou will fall down and worship me. Then saith Jesus unto him, Get thee hence, Satan: for it is written, Thou shalt worship the Lord thy God, and him only shalt thou serve."* *Worship* in this passage is translated from the Greek word *proskuneo*, which means "to prostrate in reverence to." Its meaning is similar to the Hebrew word *sagad*, translated as "worship" in most of the Old Testament instances; it means "to prostrate oneself," "to bend or crouch or stoop," or "to humble oneself."

Sagad is a physical act in worship that shows respect. For instance, the youth in some foreign countries honor an elder or someone in authority with physical reverence by bowing down and prostrating themselves in homage to that leader. During medieval times, this physical reverence was often required when approaching a king or some sort of royalty. A biblical example is given in Daniel 3:10-11:

> *Thou, O king, hast made a decree, that every man that shall hear the sound of the cornet, flute, harp, sackbut, psaltery, and dulcimer, and all kinds of musick, shall **fall down** and **worship** the golden image: and whoso **falleth not down** and **worshippeth**, that he should cast into midst of a burning fiery furnace.*

Nebuchadnezzar was not a godly king. However, he knew the vital importance of the *sagad* approach of worship. He used it to determine whether someone lived or died. Shadrach, Meshach, and Abednego refused to worship this king. This act of defiance landed them in a fiery furnace. I wonder if our lack of *sagad* (worship) could land us in the fiery furnace of hell. It is this approach to worship that the devil wanted Jesus to partake of (see Matt. 4:9). The devil knows that through this form of worship we surrender our rights and powers to whatever deity we're paying homage to. It is a statement that says we pledge allegiance, which means "loyalty to a nation, cause, or sovereign entity." During the medieval days, once a king, prince, or knight was sworn in they would make them bow down and swear an oath of loyalty. This practice is still being done till this day in certain countries. See, satan knew if he could get Jesus to bow down and worship him, he would gain access to a partial control over heaven. The principle to learn here is that as the Body of Christ spends more time on our knees in *sagad* worship toward the Lord, we will obtain more power in our lives. So, let's get on our knees and get to TAPping!

SINGING

The second form of worship is exemplified in Psalms 100:2, which tells us to "*serve* [worship] *the Lord with gladness: come before his presence with singing.*" This Scripture tells us directly how serve/worship the Lord. It's through worship by singing. We can't even approach God without this method of worship. As we reflect again on Daniel 3:10, we see where the king made a decree that anyone who heard "*the sound of the cornet, flute, harp, sackbut, psaltery, and dulcimer, and all kinds of musick shall fall down and worship the golden image.*" Notice the prophetic pattern of music first, then the physical homage of worship. Many of us approach God with prayer first. Psalms 100:2 tells us we must approach Him with singing first before we can start petitioning Him for things. To usher in His presence, singing must be applied to the communication process of approaching God. When we approach the Lord with singing, it's the best form of servanthood we can administer to Him.

Worship or to serve through this approach is the key ingredient to usher in the glory of God. In the Greek, "to serve" is the word *latreuo*, which means "to worship or minister to God" or "to do a service of a worshiper." Kings love to be entertained, especially through music. It was the spirit-filled sounds of David's harp that drove the evil spirit away from King Saul (see 1 Sam. 16:23). Much of the book of Psalms is composed of prophetic songs given to David by the Holy Spirit. These songs of David prophesied Jesus' death and resurrection. Psalms 22:16-18 says:

> *For dogs have compassed me: the assembly of the wicked have enclosed me: they **pierced my hands and my feet**. I may tell all my bones: they look and stare upon me. They*

part my garments among *them, and* cast lots *upon my vesture.*

This is a description of the crucifixion of Jesus Christ. King David was not crucified, so he wasn't referring to himself. The only person who fits these specific details in Scripture is Jesus Christ.

Another one of King David's prophetic songs was fulfilled by Jesus as He was dying on the cross at Calvary, as recorded in Matthew 27:46: *"And about the ninth hour Jesus cried with a loud voice, saying Eli, Eli, lama sabachthani? that is to say, My God, my God, why hast thou forsaken me?"* The latter part is an exact quote from one of David's songs: *"My God, my God, why hast thou forsaken me?"* (Ps. 22:1). This song was written more than several generations prior to Jesus' appearance on earth in human form. Singing to the Lord in worship ushers in the prophetic anointing. In the Hebrew, "singing" is the word *shir*, meaning "to sing."

There is power in songs. Music and singing are the main tools for ushering in God's presence and the best way of serving Him. Hebrews 2:12 tells us, *"I will declare thy name unto my brethren, in the midst of the church will I sing praise unto thee."* Every church needs to be a church of praise and singing to the Lord. Remember, the Lord inhabits the praises of His people (see Ps. 22:3). We must make praise our habit, not our hobby. When we praise and then worship, we are ministering to God as a congregation. Often, people don't understand that the Lord loves to be ministered to. When we sing to the Lord in worship, it draws angelic activity. The devil (lucifer) knew this principle all too well and used this principle to lure the fallen angels in heaven to follow him. We must follow this principle of worship as well to activate angelic activity in our lives.

JUDGMENT IN WORSHIP

Remember, in worship we judge ourselves and our conduct before we come before the Lord's presence. When we do enter into His presence, conviction takes place because of the areas we forgot to judge.

Conviction is judgment through God's grace. When someone gets sentenced to prison, he has already been *convicted* of a crime. It may not seem like it, but conviction is good judgment. Grace is the probation period before the final judgment. We are saved by grace through faith, right? However, what are we saved from? You guessed it—sudden judgment. That's why we can come boldly to God's throne through worship asking for grace in a time of need. God is the lover of our soul, but He is also the judge of it. We must remember that every time we approach the judge we are being judged, not condemned. Trust me, it's a big difference. Worship the Lord in spirit and truth, and we will have the freedom from the prison of sin and lack. When we worship in spirit, that's the intimacy part; but to worship in truth, judgment of oneself must take place through the process of us seeking His face. So, let's TAP.

> *I pray right now, in the name of Jesus, the Son of righteousness, that everyone who reads these approaches to worship shall receive healing in their bodies in Jesus Christ's holy name. May they become sanctified worshipers and grow in intimacy with the bridegroom (Jesus) in a more intense way. Let the sweet smelling aroma of worship come from each person's lips as he or she reads this. In Jesus' name we pray!*

Chapter 6

THE ISRAEL PRINCIPLES

WHAT IS ISRAEL?

The word *Israel* is a transliteration of the Hebrew word *Yisrael*, representing the phrase "the prince that prevailed with God." It's also another name for Jacob and his descendants. This name was given to Jacob after he wrestled with the angel in Genesis 32:28: *"And he said, Thy name shall be called no more Jacob, but Israel: for as a prince hast thou power with God and with men, and hast prevailed."* It became the collective national name of Jacob's twelve sons, or the twelve tribes. It was later used in a narrower sense as the title of the northern kingdom, differentiating it from Judah, the southern kingdom. After the Babylonian captivity, the returning exiles designated Israel as the name of their nation. Israel is the apple of God's eye, and it would be foolish not to focus on what God's eye is upon.

Israel is a nation where the grandson of Abraham, Jacob, revisited in 1909 B.C.. It was later enslaved by the Egyptian Empire. This anti-Semitic policy led the children of Israel into a four-hundred-year oppression. In the spring of 1446 B.C., the children of promise received their exodus from Egypt. By the summer of 1446 B.C., the children of Israel reached Mount Sinai and a covenant was given to Moses. This was called the Torah or Mosaic Law. In this law, God established the rules and guidelines that the people of that nation had to follow to obtain and keep the promise. The law that was created for the children of Israel was just a shadow of what was to come when the Messiah arrived. The Messiah would come and fulfill the whole covenant. Israel is not just a land but a covenant promise between God and His people. The next section of the book allows the reader to discover this land and its proven promises.

THE BLESSING ATTACHED TO ISRAEL

I was seeing wonderful and glorious healings and miracles in my ministry, but I wanted to see more. I begin to watch television show archives of *It's Supernatural!* with Sid Roth on the Internet. I found a particular guest I liked to watch over and over again. His name was David Herzog; he wasn't like most ministers I had encountered. He was young and seemed down to earth, and most importantly he looked like someone I could relate to. He had such an impact on me that I purchased some books and materials he had published. He covered several topics that I had already received revelation on regarding the glory, all except for one. This one was about magnifying your ministry by supporting Israel. To *magnify* means "to increase in size; to seem more important or greater; to glorify or praise someone or something." Herzog made this claim, and I was forced to search out the principles in his statement.

I had already had a revelation about learning the Jewish heritage. However, I had not known the significance of the geographical location of Israel itself. I was under the impression that Israel had broken covenant and the church was the new Israel set up to take its place. I had no idea I was operating under the spirit of replacement theology. After listening to David Herzog, I repented and started a journey to help these native ancestors.

EMBRACING THE JEWISH CULTURE

To learn more about the Jewish heritage, I had to follow a Jewish believer in the Messiah. Even though I had Jewish ancestry in my bloodline, I still wasn't a full-blooded Jew. So Herzog was perfect, even though he's half Jewish. David was cool.

My wife, Tora, and I traveled around the United States to attend his meetings. One day we were in Dallas at one of his meetings. All of a sudden David said, "These guys follow me everywhere, and they are coming with me to Israel."

I looked at my wife and said, "I wonder who's going to pay for that ticket." However, I nodded my head in agreement and said, "Yes, I am coming!" I knew whatever I attached myself to would eventually connect itself to me.

I followed the principle of, *"As the Lord God liveth, and thy soul liveth, I will not leave thee"* (see 2 Kings 2:4). I knew that, in following David around, I would TAP into a realm of the spirit that would benefit my ministry.

It was Rosh Hashanah 2012, and David Herzog was having a "New Beginnings Festival" along with Robert Sterns, Sid Roth, and Paul Wilbur. I promised him at a meeting in San Antonio that I would go and support him. So, I flew to Sedona, Arizona and the weather was very different. It was hot in the daytime and cold at night. On one of the nights, Robert Sterns called me up out of the crowd and prophesied over me. He said, *"You keep asking, 'When am I going to be next?' But God held you for such a time as this. And in six months, get ready!"* That prophecy has come to pass, because within six months revival and financial increase broke out in our ministry.

By celebrating God's holy days with several Jewish friends and supporters of Israel, I knew this was the key ingredient to TAP into the next level of the glory.

On the last night of the conference, David said to everyone, "This is one of my friends all the way from Texas, and he is coming with us to Israel."

Again I nodded my head, and with a big smile on my face I said to myself, "Yes, I am." I knew if I just kept following the principles of being a glory chaser eventually I would strike oil. However, I had to get out of my mind that I was not pursuing man but drawing close to God. I also learned how to TAP into that same portal that was on that vessel of God. We must become students of the vein of anointing we are trying to walk in by simply following those who walk in it. Being there with Sid Roth, David Herzog, and others was a time of impartation and revelation. Tapping into the Jewish vein of anointing brought a wholeness to my spiritual walk and a covenant blessing to my ministry. I truly believe this was the missing puzzle to me entering into the fullness of this new dimension called the glory realm.

JOURNEY TO THE HOLY LAND

A couple of months before the Israel trip, I told the people in my ministry that if God wanted me to go to Israel, He would have to provide and show me signs and wonders in the heavens and the earth. It was on a Saturday in August during one of our Sabbath Day meetings that the Lord gave me a prophetic word. He said, *"There will be a natural disaster that will hit the United States at the end of October. In the months following, revival will come to your ministry."*

Our trip to Israel was scheduled around that time. Just as the Lord said, Hurricane Sandy hit the East Coast on October 29, 2012. It was considered a perfect storm. It hit Newark, New Jersey as well. It was near the airport we had to fly out of on our trip to Tel Aviv in November. I was so busy preparing for other ministry work that I had given up on the idea of going to Israel. My staff then reminded me of the prophecy I had spoken in August about the natural disaster hitting the United States at the end of October.

Several days afterward, someone gave me the rest of the money for the Israel trip. God definitely gave me a sign and made me wonder. Then my wife gave me a prophetic Scripture: *"And that repentance and remission of sin should be preached in his name among all nations, beginning at Jerusalem"* (Luke 24:47). It was exactly what the trip was all about. Repentance and remission of sins being preached in Israel and the other nations. I've noticed that many people in the church don't preach on the issues of sin. Their messages are full of what I like to call "greasy grace, laughter, tickles, and heavenly fairytales." I'm not referring to real holy laughter and the joy of the Lord or true encounters from the throne room of Heaven. I'm referring to the peachy-keen messages that gloss over the reality that we are in real demonic warfare. We cannot have Jesus miracles without first having a John the Baptist message. John's message paved the way for Jesus' miracle ministry to come. This is the principle to the miracle manifestation to be displayed. We preach grace to the church and repentance to the sinner—that's backward. We're supposed to preach grace to the sinners, so they know Jesus can save them in spite of their wrongdoing. However, we must preach repentance to the church because we know better. This was the great commission of Jesus Christ before His ascension. We must learn to follow biblical protocol.

I AM HERE, O ISRAEL

A Muslim makes a pilgrimage to Mecca at least once in his lifetime. I believe Christians should do the same with Israel. To magnify my ministry like David had mentioned, I had to understand why going to Israel would help. Then the Scripture popped into my spirit: *"Pray for the peace of Jerusalem: they shall prosper that love thee"* (Ps. 122:6). I asked myself—did I really love Israel, and if so, was I praying out of a genuine heart or just sheer principle? I then repented for my motives and actions toward this holy place. A principle won't work if we don't have the right motive for pursuing that specific desire.

When our group arrived in Israel, it was during a time of war. A lot of other tour groups had canceled their trips, but not us. When the missile alarm went off, they told us to go into the Holocaust museum, which seemed quite ironic. For two days we prayed for a cease-fire during the tour. I told Kevin Basconi, who also was a guest on the Sid Roth show, that there was going to be a cease-fire the following day. Sure enough, the very next day Channel 2 News in Israel reported that there was a cease-fire. Kevin looked at me and said, "You called it."

When we landed in Israel, an awareness of holiness hit me, in spite of the friction and conflict that surrounded us. During the trip, I felt it in my spirit to pray more for Israel. My soul kept screaming, "I am here, O Israel, I am here." There is a pulling to assist Israel once you visit. Israel is so strong that it feels like the safest of the war-torn foreign nations. I was just in Israel recently, in 2015, with a tour group with Sid Roth. While there, I was praying at the western wall and I had a visitation. Jesus came out of the wall and touched me on my forehead and said, *"I'm increasing your prayer life,"* then He went back into the wall. I was looking for a strong prophetic and healing anointing. However, the Lord was showing me that an increase in my prayer life was vital in this next season.

He was basically telling me that for anyone who came to that wall and prayed, there would be an increase in their prayer life. He showed me that this was how men and women of God in the early eighteen and nineteen hundreds and also the forties and fifties revivals were able to pray for eight to ten hours with no problem. They prayed for hours without falling to flesh factors of distraction due to the release of the spirit of prayer. The Lord was showing me that the western wall contains the prayers of anointed saints who went before us. The prophecies and prayers that they didn't live to see come to pass we now have access to. We also have access to the spirit of prayer that was upon their lives. In the natural, no human being can pray past an hour or even under an hour without the flesh taking over (see Mark 14:37-38). This is why we need the spirit of prayer. The western wall is one of those points of contact to receive that anointing. Israel is the spiritual portal to receive the spiritual tools. It is the key to help fight the spiritual battle against the devil and the flesh. It is in this place where our Lord Jesus will set up His Kingdom. I want to be there when He does. How about you?

ANGELS ASSIGNED ONCE WE ALIGN

I met some new friends while I was in Israel. These friends included James Durham and his wife, Gloria. James has a heavy seer anointing. One day he looked at me and said, *"During this trip, if no one else receives, you will. God has assigned five new angels to your ministry, and He will reveal them to you as the days go by."*

The very next morning, I walked down to the cafeteria for breakfast and saw Kevin Basconi. I went and sat down at the table with him. All of a sudden, I felt the heavy presence of God flow through my body like electrical currents—it was waves of glory.

Kevin Basconi began prophesying: "Wow, I see several angels all around you. One is for miracles, signs, and wonders. One is for money multiplication, and one is for healing."

I was so struck by the power of God that I didn't even hear the other angels he named.

Everyone who sat next to me was touched by the angels that surrounded me. Note that Kevin was not around when James prophesied about the five angels that were assigned to me. Then the very next day, bam! I got that incredible confirmation and manifestation. God is so awesome; even though I didn't see the angels myself, I felt them touch me and everyone around me felt them too.

It was the fourth day of the trip. On the previous day, Kevin had named the angels that were assigned to my ministry. However, this day was different. God started giving me the revelation for this book. I also prayed for several people's healings and they were healed. That night at dinner, several people asked me to pray for them. A couple from Australia stood out the most. I prayed for the wife, and oil started dripping from her hand. Then, she started shaking, and I told her God was giving her the spirit of counsel. She started to get loud and begin to cry.

Her friend said to me, "Do you know what you just said?"

I responded, "No, what did I say?"

She proceeded to tell me, "You mentioned the spirit of counsel. Did you know they are both actual counselors?"

"No, I did not," I responded.

Many people approached her to get some of the oil that dripped from her hand. This occurrence was yet another confirmation that I had just TAPped into an anointed principle by supporting and aligning with Israel.

On the day that we were scheduled to go to the Upper Room, we stopped by the Pool of Bethesda. Pastor James told me that I had an angel of holiness at my side. Previously, my staff and I had prayed for the spirit of holiness to be in our midst. Pastor James had just given another word of confirmation.

We went to the Upper Room. However, there were other tour groups there as well. So, we did not have a lot of time to finish the tour in there. We then decided to go to the roof of the building to finish the tour. All of a sudden, the Holy Spirit told me He was releasing an angel of rain. I immediately told David Herzog and the others.

David responded, "Cool, the angel of rain."

I asked the Lord, "What is an angel of rain?" The Lord told me it was an angel of harvest. Now note, at this time Israel was in a season of drought and needed rain. They usually received a mere two inches of rain the entire season, so the chances of rain were a million to one.

The next day, we were on our way to evangelize to the lost sheep of Israel about their Messiah. We were about to get on the bus when it started to rain. The people on the tour bus looked at me as it poured and poured.

David came to me and said, "Well, you prayed for rain. Now, pray to make it stop so we can finish this tour!" He joked.

We had arrived at our destination and were preparing to get off the bus when the rain suddenly stopped. I led more people to Jesus than anyone on the whole tour. The people repented with tears flowing from their eyes. When we returned to the bus it started to rain again. The Lord had stopped the rain so we could go win souls, and then He finished pouring out His Spirit. Remember, what happens in the natural is also happening in the spirit.

For the next several days, it rained until it started to flood. Our tour guide, Mookie, said, "I don't know what you guys did, but if a group of Americans comes to Israel and it begins to rain, then we know they are from God. If not, then we know they are not, especially in this season because we don't see rain in this season like that."

God had confirmed His word to me once again with signs following. He also confirmed to me about the other angel that was assigned to our ministry. Yes, the angel of rain. It was then I knew our ministry was being aligned to walk in the divine.

I finally arrived back in the States, and everyone was so excited to hear the stories of all I had received. I was really tired from the trip, so I rested.

We had a meeting to attend in Austin, Texas with Mahesh Chavda. When we arrived in Austin, several members of the church started to converse with us. I told them I had just returned from Israel and told them the different stories about the angels. Then the Holy Spirit told me to release the angel of rain in Austin. So, I told the people I was releasing the angel of rain to them.

Just as soon as I said that, all those who were in that circle started to smell a citrus aroma. They became drunk in the spirit. Soon after, a young lady who had been nowhere near the group came up to us with a drawing of what was going to happen in the service that night. Everyone was shocked—it was a drawing of a hand with rain falling into it. The anointing grew stronger when she revealed that picture. I laid hands on people's eyes and they started to see in the spirit, and some began to prophesy. The people felt actual rain drops fall inside the building. It wasn't visible to the human eye; however, they could physically feel it.

MAHESH PROPHECY

The man of God started teaching. Then, he stopped for a moment and began to prophesy. He turned around and looked right at me and started telling me about how I was going to write a book. He asked me the name of it.

I responded, "*TAP—The Anointed Principles of God.*"

Then Mahesh said, "Finish the book; I want a copy." He laid hands on my wife and me and said, "*You have a powerful deliverance ministry. Go forward and do great exploits.*"

It was then time to pray for the sick. There was a deaf lady standing next to me with her translator. Mahesh said to the church, "If you have the healing gift, go lay hands on the deaf and they will hear." So I turned to the lady translator and asked if I could pray for the woman who was deaf; she insisted that I pray. I prayed and her ears became hot, then she heard a popping sound. Suddenly, she was able to hear at a hundred percent. She leapt for joy; it was an instant miracle. After that miracle, we walked outside and our car was drenched with water. The funny thing is no other vehicle in the parking lot had water on it. Those who were in the meeting with us said it did not rain that day. The people were amazed at the manifestation. They knew without a shadow of a doubt that this was a manifestation of God. The people said, "I want to go to Israel next time you go."

We left Austin excited about what had happened. However, it wasn't quite over just yet.

WE REALLY DID RECEIVE

In the week after our trip to Austin, I was still not sure what I had received, or if I had received anything at all. We had already seen the eyes of the blind open, the deaf gain their hearing, the lame walk, and the diseased cured. Oil dripping from bodies and from the walls in my house, angel feathers, and gold dust appeared before my trip to Israel. However, I wanted to see more of the supernatural. Sometimes, we get so familiar with the supernatural that it starts to seem natural to us, which is good in a sense. But before we know it, the excitement diminishes. Once this happens, we then lose our spiritual hunger for more of the impossible.

The following day, my wife, mother-in-law, and daughter were all in the car after leaving a store. Suddenly, my wife's foot slipped off the brake, and she sped into oncoming traffic. The cars were coming at seventy to eighty miles per hour, so she steered into the third lane. At that moment, a car barreled directly at them from the left side. The next thing you are about to hear is nothing short of a miracle from God. Two eyewitnesses saw this happen. My mother-in-law said that time seemed to stop and everything went in slow motion. My wife screamed, "Oh my God!" Instead of hitting them, the car came through the backseat on the driver's side, went through the car, and traveled through my daughter's body. My wife saw the other car inside of our car through the rearview mirror. It then went out through the opposite side of our car and kept going. There was no damage or broken glass, not even a scratch. This was the supernatural sign I had been looking for. This was the introduction to the second assigned angel, which was the angel of miracles, signs, and wonders. This was the sign of activation of the impartation from Israel.

Then that Christmas Eve, there was a lot of traffic from last-minute shoppers out on the roads. My wife and I drove to the Humble, Texas area from the southwest side of Houston. It's about an hour's drive from where we lived. We were picking up the children of a friend so they could spend the night at our home. We left her home at 7:50 p.m.

As we drove, we played two worship songs, which were about five minutes apiece in duration. Fog covered over the windows, and my wife struggled to wipe it away. The children said they felt dizzy. They didn't know about feeling God's presence in that way. I then looked out the window and saw that our surroundings were different. I saw the sign for the exit that would take us to our street. We called the children's mother and asked her how long it had been since we left her house. She said about fifteen minutes. We told her we were already on the other side of town, up the street from our home. The children said, "That's weird!" We made it home in fifteen minutes when it normally takes an hour or more to get there.

We had actually been transported in the spirit. This had happened to us once before in Brazoria, Texas as well. I had a meeting to go to, but our GPS system said it would take an hour and forty-five minutes for us to get there. So, we began to worship. All of a sudden, a diamond dropped onto our dashboard. We were in traffic on a section of the road where there were no exits for miles. When the diamond fell, we looked around and there were no cars in sight.

The children asked, "Where did the cars go?" We told them we didn't know. We then saw a sign that read, "Next stop: Brazoria, Texas." This was our exit; the GPS had said it would take us one hour and twenty-five minutes. We were translated in the glory an hour and five minutes ahead of time. We had driven for only twenty-minutes.

Why am I telling you these stories? To show you the supernatural benefit of supporting and loving Israel. Pray for the peace of Jerusalem. God promises to bless those who bless Israel and curse those who curse them (see Gen. 12:3). Let this be more than a mere principle for us to follow; let's make it a habit, not a hobby. I really did receive, and I believe you can too. Just TAP!

> *Lord Jesus, may everyone reading this right now receive prophetic insight about supporting Israel and the Jewish people. Let us rise up and stand with them in these trying times. Let us not forget that we are grafted in and that we serve a Jewish King. May both the Jew and Gentile receive the blessings of Abraham and the new covenant promises of the Jewish Messiah Jesus Christ. Shalom, shalom, shalom!*

Chapter 7

Don't Tap Out

Dos and Don'ts

Hopefully, at this point in the book you have learned the "dos" of how to TAP. Now I will share the "don'ts" or the what-not-to-dos once we TAP. I will point out a few hindrances that keep us from entering or staying in God's presence. There are a few questions I will answer, like, "Why is staying in the presence of God is so important?" "Can we have a life outside of God?" "If we are too heavenly minded, are we no earthly good?" To answer the last question first, quite frankly I would rather be heavenly minded and no earthly good any day of the week.

Dwelling in God's presence is vitally important to our Christian walk, and here's why. Job 2:7 says, *"So went Satan forth from the presence of the Lord, and smote Job with sore boils from the sole of his foot unto his crown.*" The Lord had just given Job over to satan's hands. However, God prohibited him from killing Job. Notice that satan didn't strike Job with boils until after he departed from the presence of God. As long as we stay in God's presence, the enemy can't affect us. He must wait until we are not under the shadow of the Almighty to attack us, even if God gave him permission (see Ps. 91:1). Sickness, poverty, or demonic attack cannot penetrate our lives as long as we're under God's presence and protection.

Psalms 16:11 clearly states, *"Thou wilt shew me the path of life: in thy presence is fullness of joy; at thy right hand there are pleasures for evermore."* If we don't have fullness of joy, then we haven't been in God's presence. If we are sick or if our relationships are going sour, these are indications that there is a lack or shortage of God's presence in our lives. We must strive for His presence like Moses did: *"And he* [God] *said, My presence shall go with thee, and I will give thee rest. And he* [Moses] *said unto him, If thy presence go not with me, carry us not up hence"* (Exod. 33:14-15). This Scripture indicates that without God's presence there is no physical, mental, or spiritual rest. Moses also informed the Lord that if His presence wasn't there, he didn't want to go any further on his journey. Many of us are on a journey. However, the Lord's presence isn't with us. We see it in many churches—the buildings are being enlarged, but the anointing is decreasing. It's about quality of spirit, not about the quantity of people we can accumulate in our churches. Modern-day churches parade growth in membership and notoriety in the media world as a sign of spiritual maturity. This viewpoint is far from the requirements the Lord is looking for from us as representatives of His body.

Many churches, ministries, and synagogues around the world emphasize doctrine, theological studies, and belief systems. However, very few of these churches teach and demonstrate the practice of entering into the presence of God. This principle is key in the daily maintenance of our Christian lifestyle. We need to get back to the basics.

NO GREASY GRACE

Grace is a touchy subject that most Christians do not like to debate. I believe grace is the power not to sin, not a license to sin. Jesus did not preach grace. He just demonstrated mercy to the people. Many get God's grace and God's mercy mixed up.

One definition of grace is an extension of time granted after a set date, such as paying off a debt. Jesus paid our debt through His death. He gave us an extension of time to renew our fellowship with God the Father through accepting Him as our Savior. However, what did Jesus save us from? He saved us from sin, of course. Jesus did not save us from hell. He saved us from the power of sin that leads us to hell. God had mercy on mankind and sent His Son to give us grace.

When the removal of sin or obeying God's commandments is mentioned in the modern-day church, the first thing a person operating in excessive false grace will say is that we're operating in legalism. That person is under the spirit of compromise. Even the apostle of grace (Paul) mentions in Romans 7:12, *"Wherefore the law is holy, and the commandment holy, and just, and good."* This is a New Testament Scripture that shows the law and commandments of the old covenant are flawless, and holiness is attached to them. In another Scripture, the apostle of grace mentions, *"For we know that the law is spiritual: but I am carnal, sold under sin"* (Rom. 7:14). Apostle Paul says the law is spiritual, but we are carnal—not the law. This is another Scripture that shows the good attributes of the law in the New Testament.

Then we go further down in that passage. Apostle Paul makes a statement that sounds like a contradiction to his grace doctrine, but isn't. In Romans 7:25, he says, *"I thank God through Jesus Christ our Lord. So then with the mind I myself serve the law of God; but with the flesh the law of sin."* This verse shows us that there are two different laws Paul is referring to. Paul says with his mind he wants to serve the law of God, which is the Old Testament law. However, the flesh wants to serve the law of sin, which leads to death.

There was no New Testament in Paul's day. There was only one testament, which was the Old Testament. The second law he mentions was the law of sin, or the law of sin and death. Jesus saved us from the curse of the law (see Gal. 5:13-14). Jesus did not save us from obeying the law. That would be going against His Father's rules and word. Paul said in Romans 7:7, *"What shall we say then? Is the law sin? God forbid. Nay, I had not known sin, but by the law: for I had not known lust, except the law had said, Thou shalt not covet."*

In America, many converts get saved through the grace message, which is good. However, eighty percent still continue in sin through filthy language, fornication, adultery, and all kinds of known sin. If we decide to correct them on those issues, the first thing that comes out of their mouths is, "You can't judge me." This nonsense is caused by no one stressing that these issues are not right in the sight of God. This is the reason we have many homosexual leaders in our worship teams, legal gay marriages, children out of wedlock, kids in gangs and on drugs. Then we have pastors sitting around doing nothing to correct the problem. They either don't want to lose members or they are too afraid to offend the flesh. God loves the sinner. However, He hates the sin. If someone was to go to hell, who goes to hell—the sin or the sinner? Exactly—the sinner goes to hell, not the sin. Even though God loves the sinner, He can't go against His Word. So, the Lord will love us, but He will love us all the way to hell if we choose not to change. God's love and God's judgment are two different facets of Him. We can't take His grace for granted.

The preaching of the cross and the remission of sins is offensive to those who are perishing in sin (see 1 Cor. 1:18). We must show people where their particular transgressions are outlined in the Bible (the law). This is the reason why some people think their lifestyles are not sinful or God doesn't have an issue with them. This is the reason why we must eat the whole Lamb of God. We must know Old Testament laws to see New Testament fulfillment that Jesus died for us to have. Salvation comes only through grace by faith, not through the law. However, as grace is for salvation, God's Word (law) is for sanctification. Our spirit man is born again. However, our soul and body need to be transformed after the salvation experience. This is where the Word (law) comes into play. Paul tells us in Romans 7:7, *"What shall we say, then? Is the law sinful? Certainly not! Nevertheless, I would not have known what sin was had it not been for the law. For I would not have known what coveting really was if the law had not said, 'You shall not covet'"* (NIV). Even though we have grace, the sin issues that are found in God's Word need to be addressed. Paul was basically saying the law or God's Word is there to remind us of the sinful nature of man. The apostle of grace was saying we need to keep our flesh under subjection regardless of our new, unmerited favor.

Psalm 119:153-154 says, *"Consider mine affliction, and deliver me: for I do not forget thy law. Plead my cause, and deliver me: quicken me according to thy word."* It's through God's Word (the law) that deliverance, quickening, or revival of the spirit takes place. You say, "Prophet, that's Old Testament." Well, let's look at what Jesus said in John 15:10, *"If ye keep my commandments, ye shall abide in my love; even as I have kept my Father's commandments* [the law], *and abide in his love."* This shows us that Jesus Himself obeyed God's law.

People in the excessive false grace movement love to emphasize the Father's love over obeying His commandments. However, if there isn't true obedience, then there isn't true love. We may be in love with God, but we are not abiding in His love. To *abide* means "to remain; to conform; to comply with." When we are not obedient to God's commandments (the law), we are not in compliance with His love. The word *comply* means "to agree, to consent to, or to obey a command or wish." This definition says "obey a command." So, if we are not obeying God's principles, whether we are under grace or not we cannot claim to have the true love of God.

The message of excessive false grace has plagued the Body of Christ. It has crippled the saints and caused many of them to compromise in their walk. They have given up on pressing toward the mark of the prize of the high call (see Phil. 3:14). Isaiah 26:10 says, *"Let grace be shown to the wicked, yet will he not learn righteousness: in the land of uprightness he will deal unjustly, and will not behold the majesty of the Lord"* (NKJV). Grace does not teach us righteousness. However, it teaches us the mercy of God. During His earthly ministry, Jesus preached repentance and the Kingdom of God. He never preached grace, He just showed mercy.

Many believers want to see revival. However, they don't want to hear the message that comes with it. We can't receive the manifestation without the message. What message? The message Jesus preached to the church and the world during His earthly ministry. The same message He expects us, New Testament believers, to preach: *"Repent: for the kingdom of heaven is at hand"* (Matt. 4:17).

If that's what Jesus was called to do, why are we missing it? The church has it backward. Again, we preach grace to the church congregation and repentance to people outside the walls. In reality, we are supposed to preach grace to the sinners who don't know better and repentance to the church, because we know the truth.

Jesus exemplified this when he rebuked the Pharisees (church) of His days.

The repentance doctrine has been demonized in modern-day Christianity as a form of legalism and condemnation. Romans 8:1 states, *"There is therefore now no condemnation to them which are in Christ Jesus, who walk not after the flesh, but after the Spirit."* If someone mentions repentance and we feel condemned, then it's a possibility that we are in the flesh. If a minister delivers a message on the law or brings correction to a matter and we get offended, then we are in the flesh. If we feel offended and condemned, it's because the flesh doesn't want to die.

The Scripture says in Psalms 119:165: *"Great peace have they which love thy law: and nothing shall offend them."* When we love God's law, we shall have peace. Also, we won't be offended when the law is mentioned. In Matthew 8:4, Jesus said to a man after He healed him, *"But go thy way, shew thyself to the priest, and offer the gift that Moses commanded, for a testimony unto them."* Jesus told the man to obey the Law of Moses, because the Law of Moses is His Father's Word. Jesus didn't come to contradict His Father's Word; instead He came to bring life to it. In Matthew 5:17, Jesus said, *"Think not that I am come to destroy the law, or the prophets: I am not come to destroy, but to fulfil."* Jesus emphasized that He came to fulfill the law, not to destroy or do away with it. This was the same misinterpretation the Pharisees had about Jesus' message. They thought he was condemning the law. But in all actuality, all He was doing was bringing life to the law through His spirit (see 2 Cor. 3:6).

No one on earth, not even the saints who have already gone to heaven, was spotless enough to fulfill the whole law as Jesus did. He died so that by His true grace we could fulfill the law as well. *"That the righteousness of the law might be fulfilled in us"* (Rom. 8:4).

God wants to fulfill the righteousness of the law in us and remove the curse of the law from us.

When we accept Jesus as our Lord and Savior, we are born again. This is a regenerative work of the Holy Spirit on our human spirit. However, we are not yet saved. Even though people commonly use the word "saved" to classify themselves once they accept Jesus, the fact is this: they are born again at salvation and are being saved. When they receive Jesus, their spirits are saved—that deep, invisible place of who someone is becomes supernaturally transformed. Even though at the new birth we are saved, it's also important to note what Jesus says in Matthew 10:22—*"But he that endureth to the end shall be saved."* The finished work of Jesus on the cross took place when His earthly mission was fulfilled at the Cross. We accept this and are saved. However, our mission has only just begun. Those who ascribe to the doctrine that being born again equals salvation often see no deliverances, healings, or true salvations take place within their congregations. Being saved and being born again are actually two different things. John 3:7 says, *"Marvel not that I said unto thee, Ye must be born again."* "Born" is translated from the Greek word *anagennao,* which means "to beget again" or "begat into a new life."

To be born again means to start over as from the beginning. This has to do with time. Grace also has to do with time. When we accept Jesus as our Savior from sin, our time clock starts over. We get a brand new start to get right with God.

If Jesus' work on the cross is indeed finished, why do so many born-again Christians still sin? Philippians 2:12 tells us, *"Wherefore, my beloved, as ye have always obeyed, not as in my presence only, but now much more in my absence, work out your own salvation with fear and trembling."* Paul wrote this letter to the New Testament church in Philippi. He told them that salvation was a work in progress. So, where do we get the "once saved, always saved" doctrine? Also, where did the finished work of the cross doctrine come from? If everything was done at the cross, explain why people still suffer in certain areas that Jesus died for. The answer is, Jesus' earthly sacrifice to break the power of sin off us and to restore mankind back to Father God was done at the cross. The act of passion at the cross was a real, live example of how we, His body, should continue in His work. However, we are supposed to finish the rest of the work here on earth. This is why God sent another teacher to help us finish the work, which is the Holy Spirit (see John 14:26). If the work was done at the cross, why would God send another teacher or helper? If there was no more work to be done, why did God send a fill-in for Jesus after His resurrection? Jesus' earthly sacrifice for our atonement was finished at the cross. However, the salvation and deliverance liberation process continues on through the dispensation of the Holy Spirit. Notice in Philippians 2:12 that the process of salvation is marked with fear and trembling, not grace. People confuse God's mercy with His grace. Hebrews discusses this in depth.

Hebrews 10:28 says, *"He that despised Moses' law died without mercy under two or three witnesses."* This Scripture uses the word *mercy*, not *grace*. The word *mercy* refers to the compassion and sympathy God has for us. The next verse, Hebrews 10:29, states, *"Of how much worse punishment, do you suppose, will he be thought worthy who has trampled the Son of God underfoot, counted the blood of the covenant by which he was sanctified a common thing, and insulted the Spirit of grace?"* (NKJV). Hebrews 10:28 explains that there was no mercy under the Law of Moses. If we sinned, we died—no questions asked. However, Hebrews 10:29 tells us how much worse the punishment will be for a new covenant believer who insults the Spirit of grace. For an example, if we continue being late for work after our boss has given us many grace periods, eventually we will be written up and later fired. The same goes for God. We can take His unearned favor for granted, and then when Judgment Day comes we will get fired, literally.

Hebrews 10:26 says, *"For if we sin wilfully after that we have received the knowledge of the truth, there remaineth no more sacrifice for sins."* Once we have accepted Jesus as our Savoir from sin, we cannot turn back to what we've been delivered from. Once we know the truth, sinning willfully brings judgment. Hebrews 6:6 says, *"If they shall fall away, to renew them again unto repentance; seeing they crucify to themselves the Son of God afresh, and put Him to an open shame."* This is one of my favorite verses in the Bible. It states that we are crucifying Jesus and putting Him to shame all over again once we fall back into sin. When we sin and do not repent, Jesus has to be spat upon, beaten, whipped, crucified, and stabbed in His side all over again.

We are His body being crucified on the earth daily. Romans 8:17 says, *"And if children, then heirs; heirs of God, and joint-heirs with Christ; if so be that we suffer with him, that we may be also glorified together."*

We are joint heirs with Jesus with a promise of glory. We are equal according to this passage. We can't obtain the equal inheritance if we don't partake in the equal amount of suffering. Just ask Paul and Peter and the rest of the disciples who came after Him. So, if we suffer crucifying the flesh and picking up our crosses daily through denying self, then we will receive a glorified body with Him. The sacrificing will finally be over on that day. This Scripture uses the future tense. It outlines what God promised us if we continue in the daily routine of killing the flesh and walking in the Spirit. I would like to enlighten us with a New Testament Bible verse. Romans 6:22-23 says, *"But now being made free from sin, and become servants to God, ye have your fruit unto holiness, and the end everlasting life. For the wages of sin is death; but the gift of God is eternal life through Jesus Christ our Lord."* Let's stop paying for our death with the currency of sin and bear the fruit of holiness. Let's make Jesus our Lord. Remember, if He is not Lord of all, then He is not the Lord at all. The purpose of this chapter was not to convert people to legalism or Judaism. Remember, Jesus came with more than just grace. Jesus came with grace and truth (see John 1:17). We need to emphasis the truth just as much as we emphasis grace. The truth and only the truth will set us free. TAP!

THE EZEKIEL WARNING

Ezekiel was a priest and a prophet used by God during the dark days of Judah's seventy-year captivity in Babylon. Ezekiel's prophecies, parables, signs, and symbols dramatized and delivered God's message to His exiled people. The Israelites were dry bones in the sun. However, God would soon reassemble them and breathe life back into that nation. The Hebrew name for Ezekiel is *Yechezqel*, meaning "God strengthens" or "strengthened by God." Ezekiel's warning is located in Ezekiel 16:49, which says, *"Behold, this was the iniquity of thy sister Sodom, pride, fulness of bread, and abundance of idleness was in her and in her daughters, neither did she strengthen the hand of the poor and needy."* My prayer is that we be strengthened by this warning.

Iniquity

Ezekiel first addresses *"the iniquity of thy sister Sodom."* "Iniquity" in this passage is translated from the Hebrew word *avon*, which means "moral evil" or "guilt." In iniquity, there is no perception of right versus wrong or a sense of moral value. Intentional sinning leaves everything in disarray.

Iniquity has everything to do with our own personal characters and behavior and nothing to do with the influence of demonic forces. As I previously mentioned, the devil accuses the brethren because the brethren keep accusing him. Iniquity is self-willed and self-afflicted. It is the main cause of the trials, tribulations, poverty, and illnesses we encounter in life.

Psalms 103:2-3 says, *"Bless the Lord, O my soul, and forget not all his benefits: who forgiveth all thine iniquities; who healeth all thy diseases."* Look at the prophetic order—once iniquity is forgiven, healing takes place. This prophetic pattern also shows up in one of Isaiah's Old Testament prophecies. He describes the Messiah's atonement for the world in Isaiah 53:5: *"But he was wounded for our transgressions, he was bruised for our iniquities: the chastisement of our peace was upon him; and with his stripes we are healed."*

Do we see the prophetic pattern again? Jesus was wounded and bruised for our transgressions and iniquities first. Then the healing by His stripes took place. Both writers are clear on this point. The transgressions and iniquities are ours, not the devil's. Transgression is rebellion. In Hebrew, transgression is the word *pesha*, which means "breach of trust or rebellious act." The Greek word *parabasis* is translated as "transgression," meaning "overstepping or going aside, to disregard or violate a command." When we transgress against God, we overstep our boundaries. Jesus said in John 14:15, *"If ye love me, keep my commandments."* If we are violating the Lord's commandments and living in iniquity or transgression, then we don't love God like we profess.

Let's address another point in Isaiah 53:5, which says, *"The chastisement of our peace was upon him."* Chastisement must take place in order for us to receive peace. "Chastisement" here is translated from the Hebrew word *musar*, stemming from a word that means "to correct, discipline, punish, warn, and instruct." The burden of correcting people with a backward religiosity was laid upon Jesus. The scribes and Pharisees plotted to kill Him because they could not handle His correction.

If the Lord brought correction to the world and the children of God back then, what makes us think He would not do it now? Perhaps our iniquity has blinded us to the truth of His Word. In Second Corinthians 4:3-4, Paul tells us, *"But if our gospel be hid, it is hid to them that are lost: in whom the god of this world hath blinded the minds of them which believe not."* A lost person is a believer who has gone astray. Their minds are of the world, so that the god of this world can blind their minds. Iniquity reveals one's carnality and worldliness. *If you're a friend of the world, you're an enemy to God* (see James 4:4). Isaiah 53:5 tells us what happens when iniquity is taken care of: *"With his stripes we are healed."* Healing virtue is administered when iniquity is destroyed. Let's remove the iniquity so we can obtain the full benefits of His promise.

Pride

Now that we understand what iniquity is and the seriousness of it we can look at the rest of the Ezekiel warning. The warning outlines specific iniquities. Pride is first on the list. Pride is dangerous because it's hard to detect in oneself.

If we take the letters *e* and *p* away from the word *pride*, we get the word *rid*. Pride will *rid* us of the Lord's blessings. Take away just the letter *p* from the word *pride*, and we get the word *ride*. Pride takes us on a journey of mayhem and destruction that we won't notice until it's too late. Pride is the main element in sin that keeps people from coming to Christ and serving him. Proverbs 16:18 tells us, *"Pride goeth before destruction, and a haughty spirit before a fall."* Pride and a haughty spirit are co-laborers in the destruction and fall of mankind.

Because pride and haughtiness caused our fall, we should examine the greatest fall of all and see if there are any instances of pride found in the passage.

Let's go to Genesis 3:5-6:

*For God doth know that in the day ye eat thereof, then your eyes shall be opened, and **ye shall be as gods**, knowing good and evil. And when the woman saw that the tree was good for food, and that it was pleasant to the eyes, and a tree to be **desired to make one wise**, she took of the fruit thereof, and did eat, and gave also unto her husband with her; and he did eat.*

First, the serpent (satan) told Eve that *"ye shall be as gods."* Now, that statement was true because God had given mankind dominion to be the gods of this earth. The enemy's job is to offer us promises that are already in our contract agreement with God. So, satan twisted that very statement and sowed the seed of pride within her. This same seed of pride took root in satan before he fell, making him think he could rise above God Almighty (see Isa. 14:14). In Genesis 3:6, we see the seed of pride growing. This is what the Scripture states: *"And when the woman saw that the tree was good for food, and that it was pleasant to the eyes, and a tree to be desired to make one wise."* The devil tricked Eve into wanting to be as wise as God. Sometimes in pursuing knowledge and wisdom we can pick up a prideful spirit if we are not careful. We must have the right intentions when obtaining certain knowledge. Obtaining new information can distort our character by becoming fully persuaded that we are correct. In turn, we become defensive to anyone who opposes our theory on any matter.

When placed in the wrong hands, revelation can bring disaster. Through Eve's actions and the weakness of Adam, mankind lost their position of authority in the earth realm. Soon after, the limitations of uncovered human beings begin to emerge. When pride causes us to fall, our limitations becomes exposed and our failure becomes our reality.

Fullness of Food

Ezekiel 16:49 lists the "*fulness of bread*" as the next iniquity. The first sin mankind committed was eating a forbidden food. One of the United States' main issues is the fullness of food. The country has one of the highest obesity rates in the world. The Body of Christ suffers from a spirit of gluttony, especially in this consuming culture. We eat immoderately and we rarely fast. As a result, our sensitivity to the Spirit and our ability to hear God is hindered.

Throughout the Bible, when a country falls away from God the Lord spares the people when they fast, repent, and turn from their wicked ways. Food is meant for nourishing the body, not for over-indulging. The Lord wants us to enjoy food. However, He doesn't want us to destroy our bodies by overeating. This is the warning in Philippians 3:19: "*Whose end is destruction, whose God is their belly, and whose glory is in their shame, who mind earthly things.*" When we overeat we are making our bellies our god. We are supposed to eat to live and not live to eat. Certain foods are meant for the purpose of healing, like raw herbs, veggies, and fruits. Exodus 23:25 says, "*Worship the Lord your God, and his blessings will be on your food and water. I will take away sickness from among you*" (NIV). The Lord wants our food and water to be a blessing, not a burden. It's to be enjoyed and used as a healing agent in this land depleted of trace minerals and vital nutrients we need to survive. So remember, we have to sometimes push back the plate before it's too late. Let's not let food control our destiny.

Idleness

The next iniquity on Ezekiel's list is an "*abundance of idleness*" (Ezek. 16:49). The word *idle* means "lazy and useless," "inactive and unemployed," "slow speed, and out of gear." When we are idle, we slow the flow of our blessings. We fall out of gear and out of tune with God. At that point our journey of discovering the unseen world comes to a standstill. The motion of the Spirit comes to a complete halt when there is idle time. Idle time is the devil's workshop; he is working overtime to plague us with the spirit of distraction. The word *idle* in Greek is *argos,* which means "inactive" or "barren." When we're idle, we're barren, inactive, and unproductive. Idleness will abort in the natural realm the spiritual visions, dreams, and gifts that God gives us. Don't let idleness keep us from being fruitful. So, I declare that idleness be broken and aborted from our lives and destiny in Jesus' name.

Strengthen the Poor

The last warning in Ezekiel 16:49 says, *"Neither did she strengthen the hand of the poor and needy."* Most people know that the poor need to be fed. Even non-Christian organizations understand this concept. However, if we merely feed the poor, we are not strengthening them. Instead, we strengthen their co-dependence on man's aid and not God's divine provision. The Lord does use man to assist in helping those in need. However, He wants us to assist, not cripple. The Scripture says to strengthen the hand of the poor, not just feed them. How do we strengthen the poor? We can empower them through education and job opportunities, teach them biblical financial principles, and treat them as first-class citizens, not hopeless charity cases.

The Bible clearly states in Proverbs 14:20, *"The poor is hated even of his own neighbour: but the rich hath many friends."* We must treat the poor and needy with the same respect and honor as a rich person. Touching the poor is first on the Holy Spirit's priority list when He anoints us. Jesus said in Luke 4:18, *"The Spirit of the Lord is upon me, because he hath anointed me to preach the gospel to the poor."* The Spirit of the Lord anointed Jesus so He could preach to the poor.

It was never God's intention for His people to be poor. So, before we can heal the brokenhearted, recover sight to the blind, and set the oppressed free, we must first address the poverty issues. When people mention prosperity gospel they are absolutely right. That's a complement, not an insult. The first thing the Holy Spirit anointed us for is to spread the good news, which means gospel, to poor people. What is good news to a poor man? Well, he "don't have to be in poverty no more," of course. So, from this day forward we must scream from the rooftops, "I'm a prosperity preacher!"

Poverty is a sin from the devil. Proverbs 10:15 says, *"The rich man's wealth is his strong city: the destruction of the poor is their poverty."* Poverty is a result of destruction of a person with a mentality of lack. It is never a good thing or holy thing to be poor. As a matter of fact, it's the total opposite. It really represents a curse, according to old Jewish customs and laws. Don't misunderstand what I'm saying—God definitely loves the poor. However, judgment will come to both the poor and those who wrong the poor.

Isaiah 11:4 tells us, *"But with righteousness shall he judge the poor."* The poor will be judged with righteousness. Whatever we do in this life counts in the afterlife. Jesus says in Revelation 22:12, *"And, behold, I come quickly; and my reward is with me, to give every man according as his work shall be."* Our reward in heaven will be given according to the labor we did on earth. We must help the poor and needy. However, they must also be willing to help themselves.

God will bless the hands that strengthen the hands of the poor. The Lord promises in Proverbs 28:27, *"He that giveth unto the poor shall not lack: but he that hideth his eyes shall have many a curse."* Our spiritual and financial lack will be taken away when we give to the poor. Furthermore, giving to the poor is a command, not a suggestion. When we have the power to supply a need and we don't, destruction will come to our own situations. This is what Ezekiel was trying to warn the people about. There are consequences for failing to aid the poor. If we have not received the full blessing of God's promises, we may want to consider stepping up our efforts to help those in need. Giving to the poor makes us perfect in God's eyes. It accesses the currency of heaven. Let's look at the rich young ruler.

Matthew 19:16-22 tells the whole story. Matthew 19:21 says, *"Jesus said unto him, If thou wilt be perfect, go and sell that thou hast, and give to the poor, and thou shalt have treasure in heaven: and come and follow me."* The young ruler had already kept the commandments since birth. However, through the principle of giving to the poor, this would create treasure in heaven for him. Following this principle would have perfected him in God's sight. Even though the young ruler had earthly treasures, he didn't have heavenly treasures. Heavenly treasure is not just for the life beyond; it also helps us perform supernatural exploits while on earth.

In Philippians 4:19, Paul says, *"But my God shall supply all your needs according to his riches in glory by Christ Jesus."* God's riches and treasures are in His heavenly realms ready to be purposed toward our earthly needs. Remember, treasure in heaven accesses heaven's currency into the earth. For example, Jesus accessed His heavenly account to multiply the two fishes and five loaves to feed the five thousand (see John 6:1-6).

Before Paul stated that God would supply our needs through Jesus' riches in glory, he first asked for an earthly offering in order to access that heavenly blessing. In Philippians 4:17 he says, *"Not because I desire a gift: but I desire fruit that may abound to your account."* Paul was saying that through earthly giving, those in need could withdraw Kingdom currency from heaven.

I raise the question, what do we have in our account? Is our account in the negative, or is it thriving? The banking system of heaven is in our favor when we give to the poor. The Scriptures say in Proverbs 19:17, *"He that hath pity upon the poor lendeth unto the Lord; and that which he hath given will he pay him again."* When we have pity on the poor, we give out of compassion. The word *pity* means "a feeling of compassion or sorrow for another's misfortune." Don't give to the poor for the sake of mere principles or works. Let's give out of compassion. Compassion accesses the blessings. The Scriptures say that when we do this, we lend to the Lord.

Do we know anyone who can say that they lend money to the Lord? According to Proverbs 22:7, *"The borrower is servant to the lender."* So, when we lend to God by giving to the poor. God, according to His Word, is obligated to serve us. Once this takes place, we have heaven at our disposal. Last but not least, Proverbs 19:17 tells us that what we have given will be paid back with interest. Not only do we get to access heaven, but we also get reimbursed for our initial investment with even more added to it.

In the midst of the Ezekiel warning, we can find a silver lining if we TAP through the principle of removing sin from our midst and destroying the prideful spirit. We must not over indulge with our eating; we should fast often. We also need to avoid idleness and stay busy in the Lord. Finally, we must strengthen the poor through seed sowing, education, revelation, and compassion for their needs.

TAP!

Chapter 8

BREAKING INVISIBLE WALLS

In this chapter, I will discuss some issues that need to be addressed in the Body of Christ and the world. Some people may get offended. However, others will take this as a spiritual wake-up call.

WHAT ARE WALLS?

The subject we are addressing today is about invisible walls. What are invisible walls? Well, first let me explain what these terms mean. The word *invisible* means "not capable of being seen," "not visible," or "hidden." There is a wall that most people cannot see or recognize. It's simply because that specific wall is an invisible force that blinds our intellect and spiritual discernment. Its main purpose is to be a snare in our integrity. A wall is a vertical structure used to separate or enclose an area. When there is an invisible wall in our lives, its main purpose is to close off certain areas of our lives. This prohibits the blessings of the Lord from entering in. Nothing can come in, nothing can go out. It's a structure that tries to structure our lives.

Now this structure—whether it was put up by us, our environment, social influence, cultural background, or an unknown entity—its job is to limit our capabilities. Our capacity, which is the total amount of data or information that can be processed, stored, or generated, is now hindered. A Hebrew word translated as "wall" is *gader*, which can mean "entrenchment" or "hedges." *Entrenchment* means "to dig a trench or hole for the purpose of defense." So, when we put a wall up, we obtain a defensive spirit that is digging holes into our inner man.

In First Thessalonians 5:23, we read: *"And the very God of peace sanctify you wholly; and I pray God your whole spirit and soul and body be preserved blameless unto the coming of our Lord Jesus Christ."* Wow! If a wall is an entrenchment that digs holes in our inner man because of a defensive spirit, this means the whole man is affected. Our spirit must be whole, not having holes. If there are holes in our spirit, we can no longer be blameless before the Lord. Consequently, due to the disarray of the spirit man because of this wall, our body and soul will be affected as well. Therefore, we limit our access to the heavens. The other word for wall is the word *hedges*. When used as a verb it's a synonym that means "surround, enclose, border, and bound." The invisible wall encloses us from the blessings of God and binds us to our own limited capabilities.

Some of us might still be asking the question, "What are invisible walls?" Well, let's TAP and uncover the forces that are keeping the Body of Christ and the world from being preserved blameless before the Lord—whole in spirit, soul, and body.

THE RACIAL WALL

Now, before we get uncomfortable and close the book let me first explain what I mean by *racial wall*. We are about to touch on a subject that has been one of the main walls of separation since the beginning of time. The wall I speak of has a spirit of apathy and indifference that has divided nations, families, and God's children for generations. This wall has been hidden by ignorance, denial, and negligence. Racism is the thought or belief that one race or culture is better or superior to another. The racism wall is birthed out from the spirit of division. It's bigger than a color issue. Racism is a sin problem, not a skin problem; let me explain why.

I believe this spirit of division was the first spirit that took over lucifer the archangel. This spirit caused him to grow prideful and eventually fall from heaven. Yes, pride was lucifer's main issue. However, I believe that pride was birthed out of the spirit of division. See, pride comes from division because it's a spirit that reflects on self. It causes one to be at discord with others because of selfishness. This spirit led to the first racial war between the angels who stayed faithful to God and the angels who followed lucifer (satan) and became demons. Before those demons became demons, they were once angels. Most people have different opinions about whether demons are fallen angels or not. However, the facts remains that Lucifer, which is satan, was an angel. When we have a spirit of racism, we go from being something angelic to becoming something demonic just like lucifer. When the spirit of division comes into play, the separation between different groups begins. I want to emphasize that racism is not just about color. It's about group differences of opinion on certain lifestyle choices, culture, politics, and spiritual allegiance that cause the distinction. It's an invisible wall that makes us focus on the obvious difference in color tones instead of the spiritual agenda of satan.

The race war with the angels wasn't about color differences. Remember, they were all spirit beings from God, just like we are all human beings from God. There were different shapes, sizes, and colors of angels that performed certain duties and task for the Lord. Some were messengers, some were warriors, some were just worshipers. No matter what the differences, they were all just angels. So, it wasn't a color, shape, size, or task issue; it was a sin and obedience issue. They were either with God Almighty or lucifer. So, racism is not about color; it's about causing division among God's spiritual creations. Racism is really a war between good and evil. If we can look past the skin, then we all can win.

So, racism was here before the creation of man.

When man was formed, God created a garden for him, and in that garden was a tree of the knowledge of good and evil. Within that knowledge was an understanding of the spirit of division or racism that was fought over in heaven before the fall of man. That tree was God's reminder of the betrayal that took place in heaven with another one of His created beings, the angels. Genesis 2:16-17 says:

> *And the Lord God commanded the man, saying, Of every tree in the garden thou mayest freely eat: but of the tree of the **knowledge of good and evil**, thou shall not eat of it: for in the day that thou eatest thereof **thou shalt surely die**.*

What is this knowledge of good and evil? The word *knowledge* in the New Testament is often translated from the Greek word *epignosis*, which means "recognition," "perception," or "discernment." Discernment, or discerning of spirits, is one of the gifts of the Holy

Spirit listed in First Corinthians 12:10. Knowledge is a gift of the Spirit that recognizes, perceives, or discerns a spirit whether it is good or evil. Here is my point—God did not want us to recognize, perceive, or discern that spirit of division, which is the mother of racism. God understood that once we discern or recognize that spirit, we could become partakers of its fruit. The curiosity of man's free will loves to challenge the rules of authority. This is due to the simple fact that we have freedom of choice. This is what the Lord tried to protect us from in the garden. This is also the main thing satan tries to make us recognize. He wants us to recognize our freedom of opinion and free will instead of God's will for our lives.

The reason we need the gift of discernment now is because the cat has been let out of the bag. Now, we need to know satan's plans and strategies that will cause us to repeat the fall of man. Because Christ has redeemed us back to the pure state of the garden, we need to make sure we don't repeat history, and we need to discern the voice behind the snake instead of the outer appearance of the vessel that's talking. This is the same with a person, no matter their nationality or ethnic background—we must discern the voice behind the statements they make. Once we understand that it's a spirit and learned behavior from their cultural upbringing, then we will no longer be at odds with one another's skin tone. However, we will know how to tear down the wall of separation between our fellow brothers and sisters in the Lord.

Genesis 3:5 says, *"For God doth know that in the day ye eat thereof, then your eyes shall be opened, and ye shall be as gods, knowing good and evil."* The devil's tactic was to get Eve to use her spiritual eyes to recognize that spirit of division. Once she recognized the difference, her free will began to lust after the forbidden things of God. After the sin was committed, it caused a separation between the Creator and His creation, which stemmed from the spirit of division. Then man was forced out of the garden because of it, because disobedience brings separation or division (see Gen. 3:24).

I can go through the Bible and point out historical examples of the war of racism or division—Sarah and Hagar, Isaac and Ishmael, Jacob and Esau, Egyptians and Jews, Jews and Gentiles, and the list goes on and on. That spirit has been the reason for conflict in the Middle East and across the globe since the beginning of time. The Body of Christ must break the wall of racism, or we will never see renewal, revival, or a great awakening. The wealth transfer that many people speak about will not happen until this wall is broken down for good. Proverbs 13:22 tells us, *"The wealth of the sinner is stored up for the righteous"* (NKJV). But if we, the Body of Christ, are acting as sinners due to racism, how can we then receive that transfer? Sin is from the Hebrew word *chata*, meaning "to miss the mark" or "to forfeit." When we are operating under a spirit of racism or division, the great wealth transfer will not happen. It will cause us to miss the mark and forfeit our blessings.

When there is a diverse crowd of people and one race is sitting together with their own race, as I start my meeting I politely ask everyone to get out of their chairs and sit next to someone of a different race group. I say in a joking manner, "We will do this until we all look like Neapolitan ice cream or Oreo cookies in here." The crowds laugh, and that spirit will be broken for the duration of that meeting. If we don't address this issue, we can never get delivered from it. If we don't mix the cultures and races, we indicate to God that we are still eating from the tree of the knowledge of good and evil. This breeds the spirit of division, the mother of racism. I urge every one of us not to get kicked out of our Garden of Eden because we continue eating from this tree.

With that being said, I believe that God will not pour out His Spirit on an all-black church, an all-white church, or even an all-Spanish or all-Asian church. I have found each race has their own specific anointing. We must embrace each other's differences and come into unity. Similar to what occurred in Acts 2, I believe that when all nations and tribes are assembled together and hear their native tongues being spoken, the last great move of God's Spirit will take place. This unity will pave the way for the Messiah's return. That passage of Scripture in Acts 2 is a prophetic shadow of what's to come. So get prepared, break this wall today, and let's TAP.

SOCIAL STATUS WALL

The next invisible wall that I will address is just as poisonous as the wall of racism. This wall I speak of is the wall of social status. This particular wall has no racial, cultural, economic, denominational, or ethnic barriers. It thrives of human earthly desires and material gain. These things have nothing to do with building the Kingdom. The world has been dealt an unjust hand by those who have stuffed the current images of ideal social status and popular lifestyles into our psyche. There is a burden on mankind to live up to the standards of public opinion. This wall is so outlandish that very few can obtain it. So in turn, it causes people to become social rejects.

The Lord wants to give us our heart's desires, as long as we do not take our focus away from His Kingdom business. Matthew 6:33 states, *"But seek ye first the kingdom of God, and his righteousness; and all these things shall be added unto you."* Kingdom business and God's righteousness should be our top priority. We should properly operate in accordance with these powerful principles. Seeking the Kingdom first is the anointed principle of TAPping into His divine glory. This principle helps us get our needs and wants fulfilled. We must get into position in order to receive our possessions.

Today, we seek the latest trends, fashions, styles, technology gadgets, and gimmicks while the Kingdom suffers in a tremendous way. What the Body of Christ doesn't understand is that we can be a social guru according to society's standards. However, we can become a social misfit according to God's standards. I am not advertising that God does not want us to have material blessings or even rich worldly friends. Jesus did say in Luke 16:9, *"And I say unto you, Make to yourselves friends of the mammon of unrighteousness."* We can have friends from the world but not be a friend of the world. Trust me, there is a huge difference. Joseph befriend Pharaoh, Daniel befriend king Darius, and the list goes on.

That's why Jesus also stated in Matthew 5:29, *"And if the right eye offend thee, pluck it out, and cast it from thee: for it is profitable for thee that one of thy members should perish, and not that thy whole body should be cast into hell."* Therefore, if our social lives is causing us to willfully sin, cut it out. It is not profiting us in any way. Let's not allow our personal lives to affect our spiritual walk. When we are affected by society, we are ineffective in God's Kingdom.

This wall has led to the shutdown of many churches simply because they are "on the wrong side of town." Other pastors and churches refuse to help those ministries because they are deemed unsuitable by society's point of view. However, I always say, "Know them by their fruit, not by their suit." Men and women can't find suitable mates because society says, "He must make this much money," and, "She must have a figure like this." Concern over the body image is the cause of anorexia nervosa, a disorder seen primarily in adolescent girls. This is characterized by a prolonged refusal to eat, extreme weight loss, and an abnormal fear of being obese. Hundreds of girls die each year because of this invisible wall society has built around self-image. God wants us to have recognition and material wealth. He also wants us to be healthy and walk in a spirit of excellence and prestige. However, He does not want us to steal, sleep around, fall into depression, or starve ourselves to death in order to obtain those things. Let's break the social status wall and be a true world changers, be different, be ourselves, and TAP!

THE ECONOMIC WALL

The economic wall is the third anointing killer. It's surely one of the most deadly of the walls discussed in this chapter. Economics is the science relating to the development, production, and management of material wealth. A biblical view of economics is found in Deuteronomy 8:18: *"But thou shalt remember the Lord thy God; for it is he that giveth thee power to get wealth."* I used to wonder how and why God would do this for someone like me. My ignorance of God's economic system versus the world system had me in a financial spiral for the first few years of my Christian walk.

Before I made Jesus the Lord of my life, I had the common worldly mentality. I thought that education, social status, high-paying jobs, and hard work would get me wealth. When I received the Lord into my life, I rejected that worldly mentality. I figured that Jesus wanted me to live poor in order to live holy. I didn't quite understand how or why He would give me the *"power to get wealth"* when I was supposed to be poor. The rest of the eighteenth verse in Deuteronomy 8 tells us why He wanted us wealthy: *"that he may establish his covenant which he sware unto thy fathers, as it is this day."* God has developed an economic system called "His covenant." It's through this covenant that we receive our material necessities for life and success.

The economic wall has grown higher throughout the centuries. The epidemic has become catastrophic; currency has become the point of contact in the exchange of goods and services. The power structure of the economic wall has built empires and destroyed homes all in one breath. The war between the rich and poor is another one of satan's evil devices to keep us at odds with each other. It's sad to say, but the only color that can bring the different races together is the color green. Money is not the root of evil; the lust of money or the actions to obtain it are the root of evil (see 1 Tim. 6:10). The devil has even embedded this lust for economic power in the Body of Christ.

Oftentimes, pastors, evangelists, prophets, and revivalists refuse to come to meetings or services unless there is an honorarium involved. They want to know how many people would fit in the church so they can determine the amount of the offering. What happened to the Acts 2:43-47 mind-set? When the people had all things in common, they sold their possessions and goods to help the whole community. They broke bread from house to house and were one in heart. They praised God daily, not only when they were invited out to minister, but they ministered to each other without looking for anything in return. It was because of this that God added to the church daily and many were saved.

Please don't misunderstand me. The Lord *"ordained that they which preach the gospel should live of the gospel"* (1 Cor. 9:14). It is also true that *"if we have sown unto you spiritual things, is it a great thing if we shall reap your carnal things?"* (1 Cor. 9:11). However, it costs money to do the work of ministry. I'm a firm believer in blessing those who come and minister the Gospel.

However, Paul also wrote in First Corinthians 9:16, *"For though I preach the gospel, I have nothing to glory of: for necessity is laid upon me; yea, woe is unto me, if I preach not the gospel!"* See, I believe there is woe unto those itinerant ministers who refuse to come to a city, nation, or church because of the lack of a promise that they will receive an adequate offering. If the Lord provides the means for us to go, then go. The Lord Himself told us to *"Heal the sick, cleanse the lepers, raise the dead, cast out devils: freely ye have received, freely give. Provide neither gold, nor silver, nor brass in your purses, nor scrip for your journey, neither two coats, neither shoes, nor yet staves: for the workman is worthy of his meat* [wages]" (Matt. 10:8-10). It is important to understand what the Lord Jesus was commissioning the disciples and us to do.

The struggles of traditional ministries have led the church to put a price tag on the Gospel. Pastors and leaders have taken the focus from the development and discipleship of souls to the development and growth of the church building facilities. Their main focus is on funding buildings and increasing membership. Jesus said to make disciples, not church members (see Matt. 28:19). Matthew 10:9 says not to bring anything on our journey. Matthew 10:10 says that *"the workman is worthy of his meat* [wages]." It's sad to say, but we as the body barely perform Matthew 10:8 (*"Heal the sick, cleanse the lepers, raise the dead, cast out devils"*), yet we expect a Matthew 10:10 return. If we are not fully supplying Matthew 10:8, then please don't expect the harvest discussed in Matthew 10:10. We must prove ourselves worthy of our wages. So, next time an itinerant minister asks for a high amount of money to come preach, tell them to make sure they perform Matthew 10:8 before receiving wages for their services. Let's break the stronghold of the economic wall before it breaks us.

FALSE IDENTITY AND FALSE HUMILITY WALL

What is an identity? Logically, it is the makeup of who we are as a person. According to Webster's dictionary, the meaning of the word *identity* is "the condition or state of being a specific person or thing that's recognizable as such," or "the condition or fact of being the same as something." Now that's a strong definition.

There are several key points of the definition that stick out. The first one I would like to highlight is the condition or state of being a specific person. What is a condition? A condition is the mode or state of existence of a person, thing, or circumstance. Whatever mode or state of mind we are in, that is what we will become. The Scriptures even state, *"As he thinketh in his heart, so is he"* (Prov. 23:7). We will determine our future by the way we process data.

Because our state of mind determines our future, we shouldn't focus on our future. However, we should focus on the renewing of our mind-sets. Here is another Scripture reference: *"And be not conformed to this world: but be ye transformed by the renewing of your mind, that ye may prove what is that good, and acceptable, and perfect, will of God"* (Rom. 12:2).

Before we can renew our minds with the truth, we must unlearn the lies that the devil has fed us through the years. Renewing the mind makes us prove what is the good, acceptable, and perfect will of God for our lives. This is why we must break down the invisible wall of false identity. The Body of Christ has been infected with a false humility and identity doctrine for quite some time now. The following statements are common. However, its viewpoint is an unbiblical false humility doctrine. Please realize, if we have made these statements it's not our fault. They stem from traditions of religious, social, and cultural defects. Here is the list of these statements.

- I had nothing to do with it; it was all God.
- God gets all the glory; I get no glory.
- I am nothing; He is everything.

In one sense, these statements are very true because God is everything. However, by demeaning our own identities we are giving the Body of Christ a defeated mind-set. Most will look at these statements as holy reverences to God, but it is actually an insult to Him and His relationship with His creation.

Let's begin with the statement, *"God gets all the glory."* This statement is true. However, it is also unbiblical. Romans 8:16-17 says, *"The Spirit itself beareth witness with our spirit, that we are the children of God: and if children, then heirs; heirs of God, and joint-heirs with Christ; if so be that we suffer with him, that we may be also glorified together."* Wow! This verse gives the Body of Christ their identification verification. This verse shows our union and level of authority in Christ by calling us joint heirs. It does not say all glory goes to God or is taken from God. However, it does say that we will be glorified together. God wants us to see ourselves as one with Him. This is why in John 17:22 He says, *"And the glory which thou gavest me I have given them; that they may be one, even as we are one."*

See, Jesus wants us to understand and embrace our oneness with God. Jesus said the glory that was given to Him, He has now given that glory to us. Most Christians think if they view themselves in this way, this will take some power or authority away from God. This is far from true. Many also think this type of ideology will turn into pride. Remember, lucifer wanted to be higher than God, not equal to Him; it's a big difference from what I'm explaining. Due to satan's fall from grace, many believers disown their rank or oneness with God out of fear of stepping into lucifer's shoes. However, there is a huge difference between pride and the acknowledgment of our identity in God's Kingdom. It's a big difference between thinking highly of ourselves and knowing our higher selves. Once we understand our relationship and rank with our Creator, then we will begin to see creative miracles.

First Corinthians 1:29 says, *"That no flesh should glory* [boast] *in his presence."* This form of glory was referring to boasting. Boasting and receiving glory or praise from others is not the same thing. *"Let another man praise thee, and not thine own mouth; a stranger, and not thine own lips"* (Prov. 27:2). God did not say we cannot give man any credit or glory or even praise him. However, the man himself cannot boast or glorify himself. We must let others speak of our greatness and we must keep silent and just receive it. Most of the time we as ministers of the Gospel tend to discredit our involvement in the works of God here on earth. By doing so, we send signals to the devil that we are powerless. In turn, this leaves us open for demonic retaliation. Let me explain why. Acts 19:15 says something very interesting. It reads, *"And the evil spirit answered and said, Jesus I know, and Paul I know, but who are ye?"* We see here that the demonic spirit not only knew who Jesus was, but he also knew who Paul was. This shows us that not only Jesus' name gets credit in hell for the demons' demise. It shows us that the apostle Paul was credited for their destruction as well. When we acknowledge our participation in the miraculous works of God, this puts every demon in hell on notice that we are not to be messed with.

The seven sons of Sceva tried to cast out demons in the name of Jesus. However, because they didn't have a relationship with Christ or know who they were in God, the demons used that opportunity to retaliate against them. Demons know when we don't know who we are. They can recognize if we are operating under a secondhand anointing or not. They know a believer's rank in God more than believers know themselves. The demons told Jesus, "I know who you are, the Holy One of God" (see Luke 4:34). It's sad to say, but even demons know who we are in the spirit more than we do. If our names are not famous in hell, then we are not doing our job correctly for the Kingdom of God here on earth. We must take the credit for the part we play in the destruction of satan and his kingdom. Paul said it was according to his Gospel (see 2 Tim. 2:8). The early apostles called it their doctrine that the people followed (see Acts 2:42). See, the Lord doesn't mind if His chosen vessels who labor in the doctrine and faith receive honor and credit for co-laboring in His work (see 1 Tim. 5:17).

TYPES OF GLORY

There is a difference between man's glory and God's glory. Let me break it down. Matthew 6:29 says, *"And yet I say unto you, That even Solomon in all his glory was not arrayed like one of these."* In this passage, Jesus states that King Solomon had glory. This statement didn't take away from God's divine status. However, it did showcase God's acknowledgment of man's divine authority on earth. Isaiah 42:8 says, *"I am the Lord; that is my name! I will not yield my glory to another or my praise to idols"* (NIV). Notice God said *My glory*, so this tells us there is a distinction between King Solomon's glory and God Almighty's glory. God the Father did share His glory with Jesus. John 8:54 says, *"Jesus replied, 'If I glorify myself, my glory means nothing. My Father, whom you claim as your God, is the one who glorifies me'"* (NIV). This passage shows Jesus had His own individual glory separated from the Father's glory. However, Jesus also stated that the Father glorifies Him. This tells us that even though the Father does not share His glory with another, He does glorify or boast of the glory that's upon His manifested Son. This is why Jesus mentioned Solomon's glory in Matthew 6:29 and Paul wrote about us being glorified together with Him in Romans 8:16-17. God wants us to understand our dominion as rulers or gods of this earth, just like Adam did before the fall. This was the reason the serpent was able to deceive Eve in the garden. Let me explain.

In Genesis 3:5, the serpent made Eve question her identity in God by making this statement, *"For God doth know that in the day ye eat thereof, then your eyes shall be opened, and ye shall be as gods, knowing good and evil.*" The serpent tried to convince Eve that God was keeping something from her. The serpent made her believe she didn't have oneness with God. The biggest lie was the serpent made her believe that she wasn't a god-like figure when all the while God had already given her and Adam that dominion. God had given them power to be the gods of this earth. Because Eve wasn't secure in her identity in God, He removed her dominion authority and place it into her husband's hands (see Gen. 3:16). Not knowing who we are in God or the power He has already placed in us will cause us to lose our dominion authority on earth like Adam and Eve did.

Most people (particularly religious people) would say, "Well, you're not Jesus." However, according to Scripture we are the Body of Christ (see Eph. 5:30). No one walks around separated from his own body. So, in that sense, we are one with Jesus. We are Him and He is us.

In John 14:20, Jesus says, *"At that day ye shall know that I am in the Father, and ye in me, and I in you."* Many of us have grasped the concept of Jesus in us. However, we haven't come to the understanding that we are also in Him. That is why in John 15:7 Jesus said, *"If ye abide in me, and my words abide in you, ye shall ask what ye will, and it shall be done unto you."* Once again, this stresses the point that not only is Jesus in us, but we are in Him. This could be the reason why most of us cannot get our prayers answered. It could be due to the fact that we haven't caught the revelation of "If we abide in Jesus and His word abide in us" part yet. Once we understand this principle, whatever we ask for shall be granted to us.

Jesus is the living Word inside of us. However, we are also a living word inside of Him. In the beginning, God created everything with His words. He spoke the world into existence (see Ps. 33:6; Gen. 1; Heb. 11:3). The words God spoke became living beings. We came from God's thoughts. Genesis 1:27 tells us clearly, *"So God created man in his own image, in the image of God created he him; male and female created he them.*" God planted a word-seed in mother earth and blew His breath into her, and mankind was born. Remember, we are also a word that was made flesh. That word came from the thoughts and mouth of God.

Some of us may still be wrestling with the "we are not Jesus" part. Even though that's true, we can at least agree that we have the same access, rights, and anointing as Him. Romans 8:17 states this very clearly: *"And if children, then heirs; heirs of God, and joint-heirs with Christ."* The Body of Christ has trouble walking in sonship. This is due to the fact that they cannot take this Scripture literally. We are heirs of God. An heir is a person who will inherit another's property or title. The Scripture says we are joint heirs with Christ. It is similar to a husband and wife who share a joint bank account. One party has just as much access to the account as the other.

Once again, the word *heir* means "a person who inherits another's *property* or *title*." Because we are joint heirs with Christ, is it safe to say that we share the title of *Christ* as well? I sense in the spirit that the false humility spirit wants to rise up and stone me at this point. However, to back up my theory Psalms 105:15 says, *"Do not touch My anointed ones, and do My prophets no harm"* (NKJV). The Scripture says *"anointed ones,"* and that is plural, not singular. There is more than one Christ (which means "anointed one") according to this Scripture. We are joint heirs, and that means we have the same property and title as Christ.

Having this understanding will boost our faith level and confidence of who we are in God. When this happens, we will be able to access the miracles from heaven to earth. Once we have the knowledge that we are also anointed ones of God, we will then see the heavens open. Jesus is my big Brother and my King. However, I am also a king. Revelation 1:6 tells us, "[Jesus Christ] *hath made us kings and priests unto God and his Father.*" The Body of Christ has received the priestly anointing. However, we are lagging behind in the kingly anointing. Our hearts and minds must shift to accept both positions. The priestly anointing allows people to receive from the Lord. However, the kingly anointing allows people to walk as the Lord. A cop and a robber can both have a gun. However, the one with the badge of authority will make the other one surrender. The difference between the two is the cop is connected to the government (Kingdom) of that city or state. However, the robber has limited his rights by taking what does not belong to him. The only right he (the devil) has is the right to "remain silent." Get it!

We must display our Kingdom authority and arrest (bind) the thief. The reason Jesus is called "*King Of Kings And Lord Of Lords*" (Rev. 19:16) is for the simple fact that there are other kings and other lords. Therefore, God does not mind us defining ourselves as kings and lords. Remember, King David wasn't addressed as just David, but King David.

Another belief contributing to the false identity and false humility wall is "*All of God and none of me.*" Again, we have a statement that sounds true. However, it's not biblical. John 14:12 says, "*Verily, verily, I say unto you, He that believeth on me, the works that I do shall he do also; and greater works than these shall he do; because I go unto my Father.*" Jesus acknowledges in this passage that we will be the ones doing the work, and even greater works than He did. The Lord wants us to understand and acknowledge the vital role we play as participants in the working of miracles. The Lord doesn't want us to be on the sidelines cheerleading while He's playing in the game. Unless the quarterback has an offensive line, receivers, or running backs to pass the ball to, how can that team get a touchdown? Teamwork makes the dream work. We even see this in Jesus' earthly ministry. He hired 12 assistants to help fulfill His mission. It was the disciples doing the baptism, not Jesus (see John 4:2). We must understand that there is work ethic on our part that we must fulfill.

Mark 16:20 says, *"And they went forth, and preached every where, the Lord working with them, and confirming the word with signs following."* Remember, the Lord worked *with* them, not *for* them. The Holy Spirit is called the *"Helper"* (John 14:26 NKJV). We are the ones who have to do the work; He just helps. So, when people say words like, "I had nothing to do with it," I understand their heart. However, it puts us in a useless mind-set. It makes it sound like we are puppets. A puppet does not have a voice, free will, or a choice. So, it's in no way possible that we as human beings can have an image of ourselves as a puppet. This is not how God created the human character. He wants us to feel like we partnered with Him—not just *work for* Him, but *work with* Him (see Mark 16:20). This is why He gave us free will or freedom of choice.

The Bible says in Luke 2:52, *"Jesus increased in wisdom and stature, and favour with God and man."* Through increasing in wisdom, Jesus obtained favor not only with God, but also with man. We need both. Being favored by God alone isn't enough to do Kingdom work here on earth. The fact that many don't understand the importance of favor with man in our Christian walk has hindered the flow of the Spirit for centuries. People can't wrap their minds around the fact that God has given man that much authority on earth. This is the reason they crucified Christ—because they couldn't recognize His deity. The Bible says in Acts 2:43, *"And fear came upon every soul: and many wonders and signs were done by the apostles."* This Scripture states that the apostles performed the signs and wonders. Jesus said on the cross that His work was finished (see John 19:30). So now, it is our time to do the work on earth. Jesus' earthly work is done. The true purpose of the finished work at the cross, resurrection day, and the day of Pentecost was to delegate power to His disciples. The ball is now in our court.

This notion is clarified in First Corinthians 12:4-12:

> *Now there are diversities of gifts, but the same Spirit. And there are differences of administrations, but the same Lord. And there are diversities of operations, but it is the same God which worketh all in all. But the manifestation of the Spirit is* **given to every man** *to profit withal.* **For to one is given by the Spirit** *the word of wisdom; to another the word of knowledge by the same Spirit; to another faith by the same Spirit; to another the gifts of healing by the same Spirit; to another the working of miracles; to another prophecy; to another discerning of spirits; to another divers kinds of tongues; to another the interpretation of tongues: but all these worketh that one and the selfsame Spirit,* **dividing it to every man** *severally as he will. For as the body is one, and hath many members, and all the members of that one body, being many, are one body: so also is Christ.*

This passage tells us that the manifestations or gifts of the Spirit are given to men. They are from the Spirit, but the Spirit expects us to work the gifts. One of the gifts, the *working of miracles*, is a good example of this. In First Corinthians 12:29-30, it says, *"Are all apostles? are all prophets? are all teachers? are all workers of miracles? have all the gifts of healing? do all speak with tongues? do all interpret?"* The answer is *no*. These gifts or offices are given only to certain individuals who have built up a great work ethic with God. The Holy Spirit must entrust us with specific manifestations. The Holy Spirit gives it as He wills (see 1 Cor. 12:11). The gift of the Holy Spirit is given to us freely. However, the nine manifestations of the gift of the Spirit must be entrusted to us. This increases through the work we put in with the one or two gifts He has already entrusted us with. Remember, the gift of the Spirit is free (referring to tongues). However, certain manifestations and offices require qualifications and work (see 1 Tim. 3:1-13). If this was not the case, then every believer would be walking in all the gifts of the Spirit, not just some of them.

OUR JOB

Many preachers and teachers these days don't teach that we must get qualified before we walk in certain manifestations. The Scriptures even tell us, *"Study to shew thyself approved"* (2 Tim. 2:15). This is the reason the church is powerless—because of the lack of emphasis on this principle. Just because we receive an impartation does not mean we received activation. There is a grooming process involved. Every impartation comes in seed form. However, many don't stick around long enough to see it develop in full measure. This is also why the people get discouraged and begin to follow strange fires and false moves of God. We have no one in the pulpit training them on the qualifications to get the true manifestations of God.

Paul the apostle used the word *"workers"* (1 Cor. 12:29). Jesus used this same verbiage when He sent the disciples out in Matthew 10:10; He said, *"The workman is worthy of his meat* [wages]." We are the workers; we are co-laborers with Christ. *"The harvest truly is plenteous, but the labourers are few"* (Matt. 9:37). We must stop being lazy and take personal responsibility. We must stop expecting God to do everything for us. We must work and labor in the Spirit ourselves. I'm not speaking of dead works. I'm referring to spiritual efforts to help develop and strengthen our inner man. I would like to raise this question to all my itinerant preachers, evangelists, and weekly church pastors. If we have nothing to do with the works of

God here on earth, then why do we still receive tithes, love offerings, salaries, and wages for work we supposedly didn't do? Because I said it in that way, I hope we can see how that wouldn't make sense. Again, in Matthew 10:10, Jesus told the disciples that they were worthy of receiving wages for the spiritual work that they performed in Matthew 10:8. That work was heal the sick, cleanse the lepers, raised the dead, and cast out devils. Jesus told His disciples (us) that we would do these works, not Him. The point I'm making is this—if we are not the ones doing the work, then we shouldn't accept any form of financial wages, right? I thought so. See, we are all co-labors with the Holy Spirit. He is our senior partner and we are board members in the Father's business.

We must understand that we are inseparable from God. Let's open our minds and receive the truth that we are gods. Even satan is considered in Scripture to be the god of this world (see 2 Cor. 4:4). Now if satan is acknowledged as a god in the Scriptures, why wouldn't we identify with our god-like nature? Don't we deserve that title more than him? After all, that was our position until he stole it from us during the fall of Adam. We were the gods of this world; now it's time to walk in what Christ regained for us at the cross. God Almighty dwells in us, and we are His children and not just mere humans. We, as the Body of Christ who operate under a better covenant and promises than the Old Testament saints, need to grasp who we are in God. Refuse to accept the Pharisee spirit that tries to ensnare us with false humility and false identity spirits. This spirit tries to prevent us from acknowledging our position and place in God. This is done so we won't access the power source through knowing our spiritual identity.

Psalms 82:6 reads, "*I have said, Ye are gods; and all of you are children of the most High.*" In this Old Testament Scripture, God gave us our identity in Him. It is also important to examine the following relevant New Testament Scripture found in John 10:33-35:

*The Jews answered him, saying, For a good work we stone thee not; but for blasphemy; and **because that thou, being a man, makest thyself God.** Jesus answered them, Is it not written in your law, I said, Ye are gods? If **he called them gods**, unto whom the **word of God came**, and the Scripture cannot be broken.*

Jesus was saying to the Pharisees, if the law says we are gods, then we are gods. Whoever the word comes to is considered as such. The Word of God calls us gods. Jesus was saying God's law cannot be broken; if it's in Scripture then it can't be changed. We must find ourselves in Scripture and speak our identity into existence according to the Word of God. If the Scripture says we can walk on water, then we can walk on water. If the Scripture says we can disappear and re-appear in other places, then we can do that. Never let a Pharisee spirit tell us what we can't achieve. We can do all things through Christ who strengthens us (see Phil. 4:13). When breaking the false humility and identity wall, we will begin to have unlimited access to the impossible realm.

The job of the Pharisee spirit is to get us to discredit our identity and position in God. The Pharisees didn't want to kill Jesus because of His works. They wanted to kill Him for knowing and acknowledging His identity in God (see John 10:33). Knowing what we are and who we are is the key to TAPping into heaven's resource department. Knowing that *"ye are gods"* will enable us to walk in our full calling. When we realize our identity, we will be *"conformed to the image of his Son"* (Rom. 8:29). Get ready for a new outlook on life as we break the false identity and false humility wall.

I would like to address one last false identity and false humility doctrine that has been promoted heavily to the public lately. This false identity spirit is called the *"nameless generation"* doctrine. I have heard several famous pastors, preachers, and spirit-filled bands utter this unbiblical doctrine. It is false because it goes against one of the blessings of Abraham that we Gentile believers now have access to according to Galatians 3:14. That blessing is that He will make our name great (see Gen. 12:2). Jesus wants us to be seen and heard. He wants us to be famous and well-known for His name's sake. He told us in Matthew 10:27, "*What I tell you in darkness, that speak ye in light: and what ye hear in the ear, that preach ye upon the housetops.*" Jesus Himself even boasted on earthly servants of God. Jesus said in Matthew 11:11, "*Truly I tell you, among those born of women there has not risen anyone greater then John the Baptist; yet whoever is least in the kingdom of heaven is greater than he*" (NIV). Jesus boasted on John.

The Lord doesn't want us to be shy, quiet people. He wants us to shout His Gospel from the rooftops just like John did. I heard Jentezen Franklin say that the difference between a preacher and a teacher is, "One tells it, and one yells it." We must yell the good news. What is news? *News* simply means "to broadcast, advertise, promote, proclaim, and network information from a certain source." If we are not doing that, we are not fully spreading the good news of Jesus. Matthew 5:14 says, "*Ye are the light of the world. A city that is set on an hill cannot be hid.*" So, when we say we don't want to be seen, heard, or noticed for our belief, we basically contradict what the Lord says about us. Let's break this invisible wall down.

We all have to do our part to prevent the false identity/false humility doctrine from stealing our chance to build heaven on earth. Let's search the Scriptures for ourselves to discover who we really are and TAP!

> *I pray in the name of Jesus that the invisible walls in our lives will be torn down so that we can awaken to freedom in the Spirit of God and walk in our full calling. I pray*

that you find your identity in Christ and receive the full benefits of your inheritance in God. I pray that the social, racial, economic, and false identity walls will be broken and shattered forever. May the love of God overshadow your heart toward others in Jesus' name.

Chapter 9

TIPS to TAP

The Holy Spirit told me the acronym for TIP means "The Important Principles." I am not just about to give you the anointed principles. I'm also giving you the most important ones.

SEEK GOD'S PRESENCE

The first TIP is to discern where the glory and the anointing is most present and stay there. We must become a glory chaser. Wherever the glory cloud is, we must be under it. We can't be without His presence. Develop this mind-set—if the presence is not there, I won't be there. Exodus 33:15 confirms this: *"And he said unto him, If thy presence go not with me, carry us not up hence."* Don't take a title, job, or position in the church without confirmation from the Holy Spirit. Likewise, don't enter into a relationship unless the assignment

187

is confirmed with the tangible manifestation of God's presence. A lack of His presence is a lack of His protection. Once again, Job 2:7 says, *"So went Satan forth from the presence of Lord, and smote Job with sore boils from the sole of his foot unto his crown."* The devil wasn't able to touch Job's body until he left the presence of God. We must become a presence seeker.

Some say it's not about a "feeling." My response to that is—how would we know if God is there or not without sensing His presence through the five senses of the spirit? Humans experience physical reality through the five physical senses—taste, touch, smell, sight, and hearing. When it comes to discerning God's presence, we must activate our five spiritual senses as well. Remember, without His presence, we can't receive His presents.

GIVE TO MINISTERS

The second TIP is to sow something into the life of the anointed vessel God is using to impart spiritual gifts to us. Paul clearly states in First Corinthians 9:11, *"If we have sown unto you spiritual things, is it a great thing if we shall reap your carnal things?"* Paul was saying, "We as mere men sow into you spiritual things; you don't sow into yourselves—other men do." We must understand that there are certain gifts that are imparted only through other vessels of God. We cannot receive the oil and not honor the vessel it comes in. If the vessel is broken or not there to hold the oil, then it spills and is no longer useful. When we approach giving to the men or women of God with a double mind, we immediately allow the enemy to rob us of our full inheritance. Giving to ministers is one of the ways we receive our full blessings from God.

Leviticus 23:20 tells us, *"And the priest shall wave them with the bread of the firstfruits for a wave offering before the Lord, with the two lambs: they shall be holy to the Lord for the priest."* Offerings are holy to God, but they belong to the priest. There isn't a spaceship big enough to travel to heaven and deliver our tithes and offerings to God personally. It still must be transferred through a man.

When we bless the men and women of God, the Lord begins imparting things in the spiritual realm to us through the earthly blessings. James 1:17 tells us, *"Every good gift and every perfect gift is from above."* It's our duty to bless them with our possessions to be in position to remove earthly oppositions. Let's check out Luke 8:2-3 below:

> *Certain women, which had **been healed of evil spirits and infirmities**, Mary called Magdalene, out of whom went seven devils, and Joanna the wife of Chuza Herod's steward, and Susanna, and many others, which **ministered unto him of their substance**.*

Jesus allowed people to sow into His life and ministry as these grateful women did. When Jesus delivered the women from their evil spirits and diseases, they responded by giving Him offerings. When someone takes the time to minister to us, we must minister back with our material possessions.

Let Paul's words in Second Corinthians 11:7-8 be clarified: *"Did I commit sin in humbling myself that you might be exalted, because I preached the gospel of God to you free of charge? I robbed other churches, taking wages from them to minister to you"* (NKJV). Paul poses a question: "Have I sinned by humbling myself by not taking up an offering?" Paul said, "I robbed from other churches so I wouldn't have to take anything from you Corinthians." *Robbed* in this passage is translated in the Greek as the word *sulao*, which means "exercising rights of seizure" or "to plunder and take spoils." It was Paul's right to take money from them, even charge them for the Gospel according to this Scripture. Though he had not taken money from them, he still received from other churches abroad. There are blessings with our name on them that God has put on someone's heart to be a blessing to us. However, they didn't obey. But I declare and decree every stubborn ear that didn't listen to the voice of God when they were told to bless us be reminded now in Jesus' name. I ask you, Lord, to disturb their sleep until they fulfill their commitment right now! In Jesus' name.

Paul knew that receiving offerings would give his enemies ammunition to slander him and accuse him of greed. There was a very real danger that the spreading of the Gospel would be hindered in the region because of it. However, Paul also knew that not receiving an offering from them would hinder them from receiving from the Lord. He stated, *"I preached the gospel of God to you free of charge."* If we as ministers pay the price to receive the anointing, the person receiving the impartation must pay a price as well to receive it. The anointing costs; it is not free. The cost I'm referring to is living a sacrificial lifestyle. We cannot purchase an anointing with money. However, we must pay the price through praying, fasting, and sowing sacrificial seed to open up the heavens over our lives.

Giving to the anointed vessels and allowing them to give to us will unlock the supernatural in our lives. By doing this, we avoid robbing those who give and hindering those who haven't given.

INHALE THE SPIRIT

Here's the third TIP—learn to inhale the atmosphere. One of the definitions of *atmosphere* is "a predominant mood or feeling." When God's presence is in the atmosphere, using breathing techniques can allow His presence to better enter our systems. This theory doesn't have much scriptural backing. However, John 20:22 says, *"And when he had said this, he breathed on them, and saith unto them, Receive ye the Holy Ghost."* Every time I inhale the atmosphere of the Spirit, I receive a stronger sense of God's glory. Jesus urged the disciples to inhale or receive the breath of God's Spirit. When Jesus took His last breath, he uttered these words: *"Father, into your hands I commit my spirit.' When he had said this, he breathed his last"* (Luke 23:46 NIV). So, when Jesus left the earth he released His breath (spirit) to Father God. Then, upon His resurrection, he retrieved back His last breath (spirit) from the Father in heaven, then released it to the disciples back on earth. The disciples now had a part of Jesus in them through impartation of His last breath. When we receive salvation, we too receive Jesus' last breath and also His resurrection breath that He breathed on the disciples.

The most frequent translation of *spirit* is from the Hebrew word *ruach*, which means "breath, wind, inspiration, or exhalation." Thus, the spirit realm has something to do with breathing and exhaling. When we inhale and exhale deeply in a meeting, we receive or take in the spirit of that meeting. Often, yawning is contagious, and just like yawning the spirit is contagious as well. Once we release it into the atmosphere, everyone can catch it. The devil may be the prince of the air. However, God is the creator of it. Genesis 2:7 says, *"And the Lord God formed man of the dust of the ground, and breathed into his nostrils the breath of life; and man became a living soul."* God gave life by blowing the breath of His Spirit into the nostrils of man. Therefore, when we need a fresh word or a fresh anointing, when we inhale God's breath or Spirit it will give us new life, just as it was at the beginning. We will become a new living soul. TAP!

LIVE SACRIFICIALLY

This fourth principle is one of the most important TIPS to TAP. In fact, it sums up the whole book. The principle I speak of is the principle of sacrificial living. Throughout the Old Testament and even in the New Testament, God always answered the people when sacrifices were made. After the fall of mankind and even before the Law of Moses, sacrifices were primarily "gifts" offered to God as a way of connecting with Him. The system of sacrifices was set up during the Mosaic period. Sacrifices became functions of receiving forgiveness of sin and dedicating the giving of gifts. Still, the main purpose of sacrifices was to bring communication between God and man. Jesus became the ultimate sacrifice for forgiveness. He restored the relationship between the Father and all mankind. We clearly see this in Hebrews 9.

In Revelation 5:12 we read, *"Worthy is the Lamb that was slain to receive power, and riches, and wisdom, and strength, and honour, and glory, and blessing."* The Book of Revelation frequently refers to Jesus as the Lamb. He is the sacrifice used to make atonement and amends for sins. Jesus was the greatest sacrificial Lamb there ever was. Jesus also lived a sacrificial lifestyle on earth. However, He wants us to continue this practice. In Matthew 16:24, Jesus clearly states this important principle: *"If any man will come after me, let him deny himself, and take up his cross, and follow me."* Denying oneself is the initial step. Denying ourselves means refusing to partake in something we desire. This process of denial makes us *selfless*, not *selfish*. We channel our focus toward others when we deny ourselves.

When we do this, we will access the ultimate power of love. We must sacrifice ourselves for others in order to obtain the power of love. Jesus demonstrated this love on the cross. He tells us in

John 15:13, *"Greater love hath no man than this, that a man lay down his life for his friends."* We haven't mastered the love walk until we are willing to lay down our lives for others. Jesus embraced the cross. We must follow the same pattern. Jesus tells us in Matthew 16:24 to deny ourselves, take up our crosses, and follow Him. We must take up our cross, not run from it. One day the Holy Spirit told me, *"If I have to drag you to the cross, it means you don't want to be crucified. You don't want to die to the flesh."* After He spoke this to me, heavenly electricity went through my body. I cried uncontrollably for days because of this word. Dying to self-will, selfish ambitions, and self-gratification is the highest form of worship to God.

Romans 12:1 tells us, *"I beseech you therefore, brethren, by the mercies of God, that ye present your bodies as a living sacrifice, holy, acceptable unto God, which is your reasonable service."* The sacrifice of the body or the flesh is referring to fasting, praying, and denying ourselves of worldly pleasures. A sacrificial lifestyle is our reasonable duty.

The Lord doesn't want us to go overboard with a sacrificial lifestyle. However, He wants us to make it a habit, not a hobby. This is the least we can and should do. Let's not break this habit, because it will bring us extraordinary benefits. Revelation 5:12 says, *"The Lamb that was slain to receive power, and riches, and wisdom, and strength, and honour, and glory, and blessing."*

This Scripture shows us the benefits of being a sacrificial lamb. It says that *"the Lamb that was slain to receive."* We can receive power, riches, wisdom, strength, honor, glory, and blessings from the Lord once we become a sacrificial lamb. In John 21:15, the Lamb Jesus says to Simon Peter, *"Lovest thou me more than these? He saith unto him, Yea, Lord; thou knowest that I love thee. He saith unto him, Feed my lambs."* Jesus is speaking of His followers (us) as lambs, sacrificial beings for God. Remember, Jesus is not the only lamb of God—so are we.

The apostle Paul quotes Psalms 44:22 in Romans 8:36: *"As it is written, For thy sake we are killed all the day long; we are accounted as sheep for the slaughter."* Paul is describing the war between the flesh and spirit. We must live sacrificial lifestyles on a daily basis and be *"killed all the day long."* We must deny our flesh so our spirit man can dominate our lives. Once again, this must be a habit, not just a hobby.

Paul speaks of self-sacrifice again in First Corinthians 15:31: *"I protest by your rejoicing which I have in Christ Jesus our Lord, I die daily."* We must die daily to our fleshly desires by denying ourselves. If we do not wake up with the funeral of the flesh on our minds, then we will perish physically and spiritually. Every day, I wake up with a holy suicidal spirit that wants to kill the flesh of Shawn Morris the man so that the prophet in me can live. Cut away the layers of flesh that deny us access to the spirit world.

We must kill the flesh before it kills us. This sacrificial life could also be called the survival of the fittest. What it all boils down to is, kill or be killed. Romans 8:13 tells us, *"For if ye live after the flesh, ye shall die: but if ye through the Spirit do mortify the deeds of the body, ye shall live."* *Mortify* means "to destroy strength." We need to destroy the strength of the flesh to prevent strongholds from arising. When we live sacrificially by dwelling in the spirit and killing the flesh, we can regain the keys that unlock the heavens.

We must remember that the lust of the flesh is the problem, not us. We don't own those fleshly desires and thoughts. Remember, our fleshly sinful nature does. The enemy can't attack you if he has nothing to attach to. We have access to the Helper when we deny and remove the flesh. Supernatural occurrences begin to manifest.

The last and most important key to sacrificial living is maintaining a broken spirit. This is more than a mere principle. All of God's children need to practice this lifestyle.

There are several instances in Scripture that show us the importance of being broken. One example is the passage in Psalms 51:17, which states: *"The sacrifices of God are a broken spirit: a broken and contrite heart, O God, thou wilt not despise."* A broken spirit is the key to revival. We want miracles, signs, and wonders, but God wants a broken spirit. We can fast and give our best financial offerings. However, the Lord is looking for a broken spirit above all. All over the world, churches and ministries hold meetings and receive healings and breakthroughs for their own personal gain. However, we rarely see broken people approaching the altar and seeking the Lord. Manifestations are for our benefit, but a broken spirit is for God's benefit. This shows the sincerity of those who serve Him.

When we implement this principle, we will unlock spiritual blessings. God promises us this result. Psalms 51:19 says, *"Then shalt thou be pleased with the sacrifices of righteousness, with burnt offering and whole burnt offering: then shall they offer bullocks upon thine altar."* Once we offer a broken spirit up to God, He will honor the rest of our sacrifices. A study of past revivals and moves of God's Spirit will reveal a common ingredient. That ingredient, my friend, is a broken spirit.

Many people desire an infilling of the spirit. However, they don't want to experience an outpouring. In Joel 2:12, the Scripture says, *"Therefore also now, saith the Lord, turn ye even to me with all your heart, and with fasting, and with weeping, and with mourning."* We must come before the Lord with all our heart. The Lord wants to deal with our heart issues. When we come before God with weeping and mourning, we can gain access to the throne room with ease. The weeping symbolizes our sorrow over our sins. Mourning represents the dying of the flesh. Whenever there is mourning, something is surely dying. So when I feel dry spiritually, I always remember what the Lord told me: *"Shawn, if I have to drag you to the cross, you don't want to be crucified.*" We need to embrace our cross like Christ, put ourselves on the altar of brokenness, and come before the mercy seat of the Lord through sacrificial living. Become the sacrificial lamb and TAP.

ASK, SEEK, KNOCK

The last TIP shows us that there are three steps to entering into God's presence. These steps are the holy trinity of all the principles—ask, seek, knock. All three dimensions of entry into the spirit realm are summed up in the first step of penetrating the spirit world, which is *ask*. One translation of the word *ask* is the Hebrew word *shaal,* which means "to inquire" or "to consult or demand." When we begin to ask the Lord for something, we must use strong verbal gestures. We must have a diligent attitude to be heard.

Most people don't like to ask for anything. Some may feel that they are wasting God's time. If we inquire about things that we think are small in His sight, we will see a quicker result. There is a saying—a closed mouth doesn't get fed. This statement is true on all fronts. James 4:2 says, *"You desire but do not have, so you kill. You covet but you cannot get what you want, so you quarrel and fight. You do not have because you do not ask God"* (NIV). We limit our own blessings by not asking God enough. It's not the devil that blocks us from receiving abundance. It's our lack of communication with God that hinders us. Starting today, begin to ask God for the smallest things, and watch manifestations appear like never before.

The next step is *seek*. The word *seek* is the Hebrew word *baqash,* which means "to beg, to plead" or "to pursue or search." I love this step because it requires a little more effort on our part. The majority of the world wants God to come running after them.

They want Him to prove that He is real before they believe or even serve Him. However, God is not the predator; instead, He is the prey. This is why we must pray, so we may eat of Him. Jesus is the bread of life, and we must partake of Him in order for us to live forever (see John 6:22-53). Pardon the vernacular, but the Lord is similar to a "player." (*Similar* means resembling without being identical.) See, I understand the nature of a player—I was once one myself. A player does not chase after an individual. The individual usually chases after them. Don't misunderstand what I am saying, ladies and gentlemen. I am not saying the Lord *is* a player. However, He has a similar approach when it comes to relationships. In Scripture, He says, "*draw nigh to God, and he will draw nigh to you*" (James 4:8). God wants to be sought after. He wants to be chased. He won't move until we move. We must woo God into an intimate conversation while we are in the seeking realm.

Even those who move in the glory realm love to emphasize resting in the Lord over striving. Resting in the Lord is important, but we must also remember that striving or seeking is necessary to enter into that rest. Hebrews 4:11 says, "*Let us labour therefore to enter into that rest.*" The "rest" doctrine has crippled the Body of Christ and created believers who are too lazy to contend for the faith. The Bible even says in Philippians 3:14, "*I press toward the mark for the prize of the high calling of God in Christ Jesus.*" If we don't press in the spirit, we will never see the prize of the high calling of God. We must build up our spiritual muscle by pressing forward in the natural as well. During Moses' earthly ministry, there were times when God fought for the Israelites through His sovereign touch of anointing. Then, there were times when the children of Israel had to fight for themselves in the physical realm while the Lord backed them up in the spirit. Taking action in the physical gets God's attention. It's all a part of the seeking realm.

In Proverbs 18:22, we see that the husband must "find" the wife. This shows us that God does get involved until we do our part first. The man finds the wife, not God, and once the man does his part, then God steps in and gives favor. While the husband is seeking for the wife, the bride is actually preparing for her husband during this "seeking" process. The wife must lure the husband with her beauty before she is chosen as a bride. Seeking the Lord in worship, prayer, fasting, and total obedience is the only way to get beautified. Many of us are believers, but not seekers. Mere belief in God can't keep our faith intact. Remember, even the demons believe there is a God. So just simple belief is not enough. We have to seek out what we believe in. If we do not, after a certain length of time the faith of many believers starts to waver. Often, this happens because God doesn't manifest a prayer request in the time frame that believer was expecting. This shaky faith is bred by a lack of seeking Him. After the asking realm is entered, the seeking realm becomes the most vital principle. In the seeking journey, we will learn the map to the Holy of Holies. Remember, God is a rewarder for those who seek Him diligently (see Heb. 11:6).

The final step in the holy trinity of principles is to *knock*. The knocking realm opens the door to a new dimension in the spirit. Matthew 7:7 says, *"Ask, and it shall be given you; seek, and ye shall find; knock, and it shall be opened unto you."* We may be given an answer after we ask for it, but that doesn't mean we possess it quite yet. Asking is the invitation to the treasure hunt. That's why the seeking level follows behind it.

As I mentioned earlier, the seeking realm provides the map that we use to locate the treasure. It is the knocking that finally opens up the door or treasure box that we find. Knocking is the final principle of entry needed to obtain the splendor of the riches of God's glory. God wants to bless His people. However, we must follow these principles in order to gain access to the assets of His Kingdom. Here is an application of the knocking realm in Scripture: *"Then shalt thou call, and the Lord shall answer; thou shalt cry, and he shall say, Here I am"* (Isa. 58:9).

When we ask God, He answers. When we cry out, He will say, "Here I am." If one of our children is calling our name from upstairs, we may answer, "What do you want?" Yet we may decide not to move from where we are. However, if one of our children cries out or screams, we will drop what we're doing, rush to him or her, and say, "Here I am." If someone calls our phone, we may not answer right away. However, if that certain someone keeps dialing our number, eventually we will pick up. Then if the situation is serious enough, we will say, "I'm on my way." That's what happens between the believer and God in the knocking realm.

The Body of Christ needs to learn how to cry out to the Lord. Crying out is knocking on the door with repeated force. In the knocking realm, we gain God's undivided attention and force His hand to aid us in our request. I often tell people as a joke, "Don't knock the knockers."

Once we apply all three of these steps—ask, seek, and knock—we will find ourselves living under an open heaven where nothing is impossible. So, let's TAP.

> *I pray in the name of Jesus Christ that everyone receives revelation through the principles explained in this book. May the glory, the anointing, and the power of God touch each individual who reads this book. I command bodies to be healed right now in the mighty name of Jesus. Creative miracles, manifest. And finally, may the impartation to*

move in the miraculous be released now! In Jesus' name, it is done. We have TAPped!

TAP!

About Shawn Morris

Shawn Morris is a dynamic and anointed minister of the gospel who operates in a remarkable prophetic, healing, miracles, signs and wonders anointing. He is a mentor to hundreds of pastors and ministers across the world. He is also the president and founder of Shawn Morris International Ministries in Houston, Texas. As an international evangelist, Shawn and his wife have led thousands to Christ and have been catalysts for releasing small town revivals across the country. The Morrises reside in Houston, Texas with their eight children.

Contact Shawn Morris

Email me at: prophet@shawnmorris.org

For booking contact us at 281-818-6982.

Send all donation and tax deductible gifts to:

P.O. Box 1802 Alief, Texas 77411.

You can also donate online at: www.shawnmorris.org.